10 POWERFUL STRATEGIES FOR CONFLICT DE-ESCALATION

HOW TO ACHIEVE CONFLICT RESOLUTION THROUGH EFFECTIVE COMMUNICATION

SIMON OSAMOH

© **Copyright 2022 - All rights reserved.**

The content contained within this book may not be reproduced, duplicated, or transmitted without direct written permission from the author or the publisher.

Under no circumstances will any blame or legal responsibility be held against the publisher, or author, for any damages, reparation, or monetary loss due to the information contained within this book, either directly or indirectly.

Legal Notice:

This book is copyright protected. It is only for personal use. You cannot amend, distribute, sell, use, quote, or paraphrase any part, or the content within this book, without the author or publisher's permission.

Disclaimer Notice:

Please note that the information contained within this document is for educational and entertainment purposes only. All effort has been executed to present accurate, up-to-date, reliable, complete information. No warranties of any kind are declared or implied. Readers acknowledge that the author is not rendering legal, financial, medical, or professional advice. The content within this book has been derived from various sources. Please consult a licensed professional before attempting any techniques outlined in this book.

By reading this document, the reader agrees that under no circumstances is the author responsible for any losses, direct or indirect, that are incurred due to the use of the information in this document, including, but not limited to, errors, omissions, or inaccuracies.

CONTENTS

Preface   5

STRATEGY ONE - GIVE POSITIVE
CHOICES   13
Conflict of speaking in public   17
Positive Choices   21

STRATEGY TWO - KNOW THE TYPES
OF ANGER   27
Avoidance   28
Forceful   31
Collaborative   33
Indirect control   34
Radical Reaching Out   36

STRATEGY THREE - MANAGE THE
ANGER   39
High jinks with my son   41
Kickboxing fight over a broken light?   46

STRATEGY FOUR - FIND THE VOICE
OF REASON   49
Determining the personality type   49
Habits of logic-dominant people   58
Habits of value-dominant people   61
"I'm going to hurt people today"   63
Key learning   66

STRATEGY FIVE - USE YOUR BODY
AND VOICE   69
Being bold in finding compliance   81

STRATEGY SIX - ACTIVE LISTENING/DISTRACTION	85
Active Listening	86
STRATEGY SEVEN - FOSTER GOOD CONVERSATIONS	93
What it took to tackle "problem" kids	108
STRATEGY EIGHT - REMOVE COMMUNICATION BARRIERS	113
The Churchman, the Gang, and the Cop	121
STRATEGY NINE - REMEMBER PERSONAL SAFETY	129
Jim – and the stranger in the church	130
A very angry young man – and me	133
STRATEGY TEN- KNOW IF YOU'RE THE RIGHT PERSON	143
Frank was the right person at the right time	147
Epilogue	153
About the Author	157

PREFACE

It seems fitting that before you get into the 10 powerful strategies on conflict resolution that I tell you a little bit about my background and how I became an expert in this field.

I'll start with my police career, I joined the police at 19 years old and served 14 years in Thames Valley Police in England, spending most of my time as a detective focused on organized crime. Thames Valley has around 4,000 officers and a couple thousand support staff. In the UK, we don't have federal law enforcement so it's a police department made up of many different specialties. When I left in 2011 after 14 years' service to emigrate to America, I was working in the organized crime covert ops division.

I worked on many notable high-profile cases at this time, one being the "Liquid bomb terrorism plot" in 2006 with the British security services. This case changed aviation security worldwide, limiting the amount of liquid that can be taken on planes. In those 14 years, I was honored to be commended by the chief of police on many occasions for investigative work. At least four of those commendations revolved around dealing with extreme conflict or being able to defuse disputes in some way. I've spent time in community policing, robbery teams, burglary teams and have

investigated crimes such as rapes, murders, and assaults. In a busy metropolitan department West of London, I saw enough people in crisis during my 14 years to last me a lifetime. My love of conflict resolution, though started a few years before I joined the police.

Before joining the police, I worked in a care home for adults with learning disabilities just outside London at a place called Binfield Park. At the time, it was an institutional center for persons with learning disabilities. At Binfield Park, someone was always "having a bad day" and conflict was all around us as members of the team. The residents were the type of people who had problems unpacking their emotions which led to arguments and conflict. The reasons for their crises were many and could range from someone simply having taken someone else's toy or a person wearing someone's else's clothes. Simple things, yes, but for those involved it was very traumatic.

It was a volatile place with many arguments. However, I was raised in a large family with two brothers and two sisters, so I knew all about conflict as with a large family we had it at home, although Binfield was on another level. It was here that I started to develop the skills that I will share with you in this book. As an 18-year-old working with people with disabilities, I learned all the skills necessary to defuse conflict and I want to empower you with those very techniques.

Empathy and understanding are key factors in conflict de-escalation that you will read about in this book. As I've said, there was a higher degree of emotional

instability in the Binfield demographic. It was here, in these situations, I learned the importance of the words I chose to speak, analyzing the stages of anger the person demonstrated and what path had taken them there.

There are four stages of anger – event triggers, escalation of emotions, breaking point, and recovery. I will discuss all these factors in the book. At Binfield, I found that certain words I used would escalate the situation. If I used other words, I would bring calm to the proceedings. What I learned at Binfield was to focus on results, things that worked. I could find out quickly what didn't work and discard them from my repertoire. It's very important to focus on the tactics that had the greatest effect and hone your skills in these areas. I'm going to teach you in this book how to act on what my experiences have taught me to employ when attempting to defuse a situation that has conflict.

I remember a resident called Henry, who was an avid snooker player *(snooker is an English version of pool just a bit more complicated!)*. I was too, so we hit it off. So, one night he came running through the lounge, where around 40 residents were watching TV, and he was shouting and screaming, the snooker cue in one hand and his fist raised in the other. He was chasing one of the other residents, who looked like he was fleeing for his life. Nobody knew what had happened.

When I saw the 5-foot snooker cue being dangerously waved around, I moved quickly and caught up with Henry and the resident he was chasing. So why did all hell break loose? It transpired that Henry was playing a game of snooker and about to win. As he walked to the table to play his *coup de gras*, he noticed the ball on the snooker table had been moved. All hell broke loose. Henry's mental disability caused him to behave like a young teen when, in fact, he was in his 40s. He did, in fact, have some sound cognitive abilities but was emotionally very immature. Emotions, then, were running high.

I suddenly found my de-escalation technique! This is the moment that I discovered the true meaning of conflict resolution – active listening, setting boundaries and giving people positive choices.

Boundaries won't work if someone is waving a long snooker cue around. I told Henry that his behavior was not acceptable, and he had to put down the snooker cue. I told him that if he didn't do that, I would have to take the cue from him. I just listened to Henry attentively without interrupting and gave him the opportunity to air his grievances. So, it all came out with wild gestures and big eyes. I let him get it all off his chest, then offered him some positive choices.

He could take his snooker cue (gently) and find someone else to play with. Or, I said, I would love to play him, but assured him I would beat him. That did the trick. The positive choice worked – I saw the competitive flame start burning in his eyes. He would obviously like to play a game than no game at all. The situation was defused just like that. The other resident was allowed to leave, and peace returned. One of the big negatives that could have happened was a stalemate, where neither side was prepared to give and take. I had seen that happen with a junior person on the team, and the situation became worse. Both the caregiver and resident were shouting at each other. Not good.

There doesn't have to be a winner and a loser in conflict resolution, and you will learn more about that in this book. When you empower the person to make positive choices, it normally always works. Offering choices is a key factor in de-escalation as you will learn later.

So, this is what I've learned about conflict that can help you! A crisis is a bit like a balloon full of air. You don't need to know who filled up the balloon. How did it get so big? Or will it get that big ever again? Your job is just to let a little air out of the balloon, just enough so it doesn't burst, and the danger is averted. Many use this technique. It is the perfect fit to conflict. One of my good friends, Dr. James Densley, criminologist and co-founder of the Violence Project, uses this methodology. The focus of conflict resolution is not to let the balloon burst but to find a way to let air out of the person, so they don't do just that. That's all you should be concerned about – finding a way to let air out of the balloon.

I have spent the last 25 plus years living and working where conflict is all around me, and through my experience I've developed 10 powerful strategies that if you can master, will help you successfully de-escalate persons who are either in conflict, agitated or in a highly charged state.

So, let's dive in!

Simon Osamoh

STRATEGY ONE - GIVE POSITIVE CHOICES

#Decision Making #Active Listener #Positive Choice #Bad Options #Empowerment

When I was Director of Risk and Compliance at Equiniti Trust company, I left my office for a meeting at a separate building. As I passed through the break room to leave, I saw a woman sitting there, her chin resting on her hands, her eyes closed.

What struck me at first is that she wasn't dressed very professionally. She looked very casual for someone about to begin the working day. She was wearing a pink top and leggings. When I came back from my meeting, around two hours later, the woman was still there. She had her head in her hands now.

I decided the best move would be to talk to the HR team to see if they knew anything about the woman who looked so distressed. The HR Director said: "I'm so happy that you're here, Simon. We've been waiting for you because we can't get the woman to leave." It transpired that she had been fired because she was always late, and because she had never dressed properly for the occasion.

After she had been terminated, she refused to leave the building. The HR Director asked me if I could ask her to leave. I went to the break room, and the woman was still there, in the same position. I went up to her and sat opposite. I explained who I was. "Hi there. I'm Simon, the Director of Risk and Compliance."

I told her that I was here to listen and asked if we could go somewhere more private, where there were no distractions. She agreed, and we went to a side room. Today, it has become the norm to have another person with you, especially if a person is from the opposite sex.

I said: "I understand that you've been terminated for never coming in on time and not being appropriately dressed. I'm here to listen to what you have to say." She told me that no one had said she couldn't wear casual clothes to work. She also said that she had a good reason for being late, but no one wanted to listen to her.

She also told me she was pregnant and was very distressed about losing her job. She said without her job, she wouldn't be able to pay her bills and was very worried about how she would cope, especially because she was pregnant. She said that she needed her job back and kept on about this.

I listened for about 15 to 20 minutes. I never interrupted. I just let her get it all off her chest. At the end of that, I said: "So you feel that you've been wrongly dismissed? There is little I can do today. I would suggest that you speak to an attorney about your dismissal being either unlawful or without good cause.

"What we have to resolve right now is that for you to accept you have been terminated and that staying here inside the building is not an option." I went on to give her two positive choices. For a newbie de-escalator, remember that you must be able to fulfill these options, otherwise there would be no trust.

"We can drive you to a bus stop where you can get a bus to wherever you need to go. Or I can call an Uber to take you home." I then gave her the bad choice: "If you decide on neither of those offers, I have no option but to call the police and you will be arrested for trespassing." The woman took the Uber offer and after about 30 minutes, she left the building. The HR Director praised me for my work and for the successful de-escalation of the crisis in the break room.

For me, this was a classic de-escalation procedure. I bring this case up often in the book and for a good reason. This routine is what you should follow when dealing with a non-violent person who has no intention of harming others or being disruptive. It was a calm environment with no other people who could have influenced her behavior. The procedure, as I said, was classic.

I demonstrated active listening, which meant:

I never spoke while she was speaking.

I gave minimal prompts like nodding while she was speaking.

It showed I was fully engaged in the conversation.

Afterward, I paraphrased what she had told me.

I then put in boundaries – she couldn't stay in the building.

I offered a way to resolve the situation by offering two good choices (taking a bus or Uber).

I gave her a bad choice (staying and then being arrested).

The situation was resolved.

I realized two things about that day. Firstly, the HR department struggled to manage the situation. Secondly, it was clear to me that if you followed a structure, a strategy, it is possible to remove conflict from situations. Empower the person by offering choices. Even in a crisis, this works.

This story is one of the reasons I created this book. There is a great need for de-escalation. There are crises such as the above and many, many more. I want you to have the same level of understanding and empowerment that I was blessed with on that day, so whenever you see conflict, whatever shape or form it may take in your business, employment, or your hobby, you'll be equipped to take the appropriate action.

CONFLICT OF SPEAKING IN PUBLIC

Vance was doomed to a lifetime of insecurity and failure because of a speech impediment. But then a de-escalator stepped into the scene.

Here's another very different situation a friend had to manage. He was called in to talk to Vance, a shy, good-looking kid who, according to the principal had a debilitating issue with speaking in public. It was an overriding fear, meaning that it consumed much of his thought.

The thing is that he was overly bright and could have been scoring straight A's in virtually anything he handled. He was, instead, failing at most everything. The school psychologist had spoken to him, but he refused to say anything. My friend was called in as a last resort.

My friend spoke to some of Vance's teachers, who all affirmed that when Vance was asked a question, he went to pieces. This was a source of great fun to the other pupils and humiliation for Vance. The teachers were becoming frustrated because they knew Vance could have answered the question with ease. They all knew that he was an exceptional student and couldn't understand what was happening.

He had been coaxed into the theatre club for a small part. One day, the director of the play said he would like all students to just say a couple of lines to the school about what they had gained from being in the play. Vance never went back. He got his mother to talk to the school about how it was interfering with his work and how he wanted to leave the theatre club. It was such a shame because he liked it and he showed talent.

My friend learned all this after talking to his parents. It took a few sessions with Vance for him to open up a little with him. He had also read up about a star employee for an IT company who was told he had to give a keynote address at a company function and promptly resigned a couple of days later. His boss just couldn't understand it. He was in line to become head of a large division and was prized at every turn.

Looking back, he remembered that he always got his assistant to lead meetings. That was the only thing about the employee that had niggled him. This was a crisis, but not one of the situations my friend was used to dealing with. It turned out that Vance wasn't always afraid of public speaking (his confession) but became terrified after a teacher many years back had derided him for his lack of eloquence in replying to a question. He said the teacher liked to belittle scholars, but the other kids had shaken it off. Not Vance. The teacher had told him he would end up sweeping the streets. He believed him.

Little by little, he opened up. My friend said: "I used all my crisis de-escalation methods even though this was not a normal situation. I listened very carefully. I indicated that I was following his story thoroughly by nodding my head and reaching out my hand gently to make a point.

After each session, I summed up what the afternoon session had delivered. In the times (the early days), when he never spoke at all because he was suspicious of me, I listened to the silence. He relaxed and just enjoyed the moment. It was important not to rush anything. Don't feel you have to speak for the sake of it.

Slowly, he began to confide in me. I offered him some positive choices. He could become an active member of the school and reap the joy of participating, not just being present. His schoolwork would improve. His chances of getting into good establishments for further learning would improve. He could become a pal and confidant to others at school that would love his friendship. Another decision was that he could just carry on as is. Did he want to look back on wasted years? This could determine his future. It was that important.

My friend wasn't telling him anything he didn't know. He was a star pupil being held back by an irrational fear loaded onto him as a burden by an irresponsible person who should never have been a teacher in the first place. It was the positive choices that swayed him. He had to hear it from him.

Deep down, of course, he knew it. But he needed to hear it. It changed his life, and he went into a very successful career after school as a – wait for it – a motivational speaker who was in high demand. My friend and Vance remained friends over the years and my friend went to one of his seminars. "Said it was incredible." His audience was enthralled. Was this the shy boy with a terrible fear? Certainly not anymore.

POSITIVE CHOICES

How it helped Philip James, a doomed man. This man was on his way to incarceration, but positive choices were available for him on the way there.

In 2006 I worked on one of the largest seizures of drugs that my police department in England had ever dealt with. Around 3 million GBP in street value of cannabis was being imported into the country via Holland each week. After a surveillance operation, we arrested several people in the south of England with large amounts of drugs concealed inside refrigerators.

Our reactive inquiries and researched phone records indicated a person in the northern part of the country was in regular contact with the supplier of the drugs in the south.

This person up north would always be in contact by phone with the person down south around the time of drug deliveries. The inference was that the person up north had to be involved as they were always in communication at the time of drug deliveries, so we took our team, headed north with a search warrant, and went to find this person. The owner of the phone was identified as Philip James. When he was arrested and all the buildings that he controlled searched, more cannabis drugs were found, some 1 million GBP of drugs ready to be distributed throughout the country.

It was obvious that Philip James never expected to be caught like so many other organized criminals. He went from living the good life, earning amazing sums of money, feeling that he was untouchable, to being arrested by a police department from 250 miles away.

Imagine if you can, a middle-class businessman who had his entire life flash before him. He knew that drugs that had been seized in the southern part of the country could be connected to him and he knew that drugs found in his house would undoubtedly put him in prison for a very long time.

So, you could say he went into crisis mode at that time, wondering what his business partners would do and say, what would his family think, and more importantly that house and businesses that he owned would be seized under the Proceeds of Crime Act 2002. You get the picture of the self-inflicted crisis he was in.

So why am I telling this story? Well, on the 250 miles journey back he was solemn, and very quiet, with a glazed look on his face as he contemplated what his future would look like. To update you on that part of the story, he got 11 years in prison for his part in the conspiracy and had his house and business assets seized, but here's how positive choices can help in your de-escalation efforts.

We had to stop for a rest break on the way back to our police headquarters. He didn't want to walk into the restaurant with handcuffs, so I gave him two positive choices and an option I knew he wouldn't want. The first option – he knew he would be going to prison for an exceptionally long time and would not be in this position again where he could (1) Walk into the restaurant as a free man with no handcuffs, without judgment from others (2) He could have one last enjoyable meal of his choosing, anything from the menu, before prison food became his master. And then the third option he had was that when the handcuffs came off and he ran, he was miles from his home, with no phone, no money, and was under arrest for a serious offence. To run and try and escape would add years to his sentence. He most probably wouldn't get very far as I could run the 100 meters at close to 14 seconds in my heyday.

Which option did Philips James take? Rightly, for a man in survival mode with his whole world turned upside down, he took a combination of options 1 and 2. I'm sure his fried chicken tasted extra nice that day knowing it would be the last time in years he would have such a meal. His demeanor changed, his body language changed, and I think we did a lot that day to show him that there was humanity even in his darkness. It pulled him out of the despair of the survival mode he had entered.

My friend Denise Koster, a workplace violence expert from Canada, has worked in the field of violence since 1985. I love a quote in her book *"Refusing to accept the unacceptable, the trials, tribulations and triumphs of workplace bullying and harassment"* by Michelle Rosenthal. It says "Survival mode is supposed to be a phase that helps you save your life. It's not meant to be how you live."

When someone is in crisis or a highly emotional state, empowering them to make the right choices might not divert the crisis, but it's my belief it will help them see reason more quickly.

Recap: Positive choices can turn a charged situation around for the better. It is the make-or-break moment that empowers the listener to override the negativity that has been a debilitating fear. It also

allows for the switching of left-brain to right-brain thinking, from the emotional to the logical, and this can prove the worthy ingredient needed to resolve the situation.

STRATEGY TWO - KNOW THE TYPES OF ANGER

#Avoidance #Forceful #Indirect Control #Collaborative #Reaching Out

At the gigantic Mall of America, in Bloomington Minnesota, I was a security manager overseeing a behavior detection program. I want to tell you a bit about the mall, I'll start by saving it is massive! It is a little over six million square feet, has around 42 million visitors each year and is actually a bigger tourist attraction than Disney because its free to get in! To add this to your imagination it has its own theme park inside including a giant roller-coaster.

So, with so many visitors safety is paramount. My former team involved a group of highly trained security practitioners who were on the lookout for unusual behavior that might have led to terrorist activity. When these security practitioners see behaviors that go against the baseline behavior of the mall, they conduct what the mall refers to as security interviewing.

In a mall this large there were plenty of instances where behavior was outside baseline that led to interviews. And undoubtedly someone would always complain about their experience and interaction with the behavior detection officers. This meant that I could spend my days dealing with highly charged complaints by people who had been spoken to by my team.

In my experience, there are four types of anger and I had to utilize conflict de-escalation to defuse volatile situations. This has been my MO for all types of hostile behavior throughout my career. Here I'm going to explain the 4 types of anger.

AVOIDANCE

These people can be reclusive, express emotions singularly, to the self, and avoid angry people. These people avoid conflict at any cost and stay away at a very safe distance. Like the myth of an ostrich burying its head in the sand, so do they.

These people hope that the anger will just disappear. They truly feel helpless around conflict and at times will go to extraordinary measures to avoid it. They find themselves at a disadvantage, as they can't get a real take on the situation. Even if somebody has wronged them, they would rather retreat than take the matter up with that person. Consequently, issues are not dealt with, but 'buried.' Unfortunately, they don't magically disappear by doing this. Just the opposite. It can lead to relationships breaking up because of the resentment and emotional turmoil that grows with time. If only the issues had been dealt with in a mature and manageable way, and if solutions had been found as a result, you can move on.

Maybe the person has not had any type of conflict in their life or has led a sheltered existence. We tend to think these people are lucky. It does not, though, give them the ability to deal with conflict later in life, and they will find plenty of it. They are, as it were, emotionally stagnant. Liken them also to a dormant volcano. This is an apt description of someone whose emotions have always been suppressed, but not vanquished. One day they will erupt, like a volcano, in an explosion which can hopefully still be dealt with via conflict resolution.

For a while, at first, with the person avoiding conflict at all costs, this attitude can defuse a situation and allow breathing space. But and this is a big but, something that happened three or four years ago that was 'buried' will rumble to the surface and will be much harder to deal with than if it had been managed properly in the first place. It could be like a dormant volcano that has suddenly become active and impossible to contain. This can lead to all sorts of devastating consequences. It just takes a trigger for this to happen – and that trigger could be anything. Many avoiders think they have resolved the problem by ignoring it. Someone more astute could try talking to them but mostly without much success.

Most of us can remember a co-worker at work who fits the avoider profile perfectly. I used to work for a company whose director, to whom I reported, said he used to dislike conflict. It was also obvious. Every decision that he made was done to avoid any kind of conflict. At the first sign of any kind of disagreement, he would avoid a situation like the plague. What he needed to do was to move right into that situation and resolve the situation before it escalated. As it was, the bitterness and anger just continued, at a lower level, but you could feel a rumbling beneath the surface. It certainly didn't make for a productive work environment.

FORCEFUL

Quite the opposite of avoidance, this person moved right into the middle of the conflict as quickly as possible. They use tactics and words that carried the full weight of the "I'm going to sort this out, right here, right now" attitude. Sometimes this comes with intimidation and threats.

This person muscles into the heart of the situation, like a Pitbull, and intimidates anyone who attempts to stop them. It's not like this person is burning with rage. They are very comfortable in this position, and it's almost as if you'd offered them a cup of coffee, which they sip while dealing out verdicts and solutions.

The advantage of this kind of behavior is that it can end conflict very quickly. However, it can also destroy relationships. If that barrage of words is aimed at an avoider, that person could withdraw even further, adding to the problem, or causing problems in the workplace that weren't there before.

The forcers know they will not be challenged because whoever does will be shouted down. They intimidate people very easily, so people feel they would rarely argue with someone like this.

So, I happened to work for a forcer, who adored conflict. At the first sign of trouble, he would stick his size 10 shoes into the situation, whether he needed to or not. This way, he would resolve the situation immediately, but he became a feared leader.

This is not conducive to productivity. People were very hesitant in sharing views and opinions with him knowing he would find fault and belittle them. If people are not encouraged, there will be no springs of innovation, no assistance, and no motivation. With the forcer, rule of law is 'my way or the highway,' and in the process could lose many fine people. If only they took the time to look at themselves, they could change for the better and, in turn, reap rich rewards for their job or role.

They could also attract some terrific people to work for them if they are a manager. No one likes being put down. If they know there is space for their opinions and ideas they will be encouraged rather than despaired, and they will flock to work for the person or company. So, the forcer may solve conflict situations but could leave a lot of broken spirits in their wake, creating new conflict. Not recommended! You may win the war but leave casualties strewn across the battlefield.

COLLABORATIVE

This person will ensure that the anger is dealt with in a positive way. These people find constructive solutions. Anger needs to be defused and channeled into something affirmative. Constructive feedback is the order of the day.

Intense conflict with heated discussions suddenly becomes positive. The temperature drops dramatically and with the collaborator, you could find yourself wondering why things were so heated in the first place.

The collaborator will make sure all sides of the story are discussed in a congenial and studied manner. There is great feedback instead of fear. People are encouraged to contribute. This is the way to build a healthy company or relationship.

When discussion is based on facts, things can be disseminated dynamically. Add reason into the mix and you could have a generously lively meeting. It should be looked forward to, not feared.

On the negative side, the collaborator could take a lot of time to sort out an issue as they are trying to give everyone a share in the discussion. They don't want to draw a line in the sand. They don't want to institute boundaries as this could cause disagreement. This person could also be hedging their bets and there could be some passive aggressiveness.

I worked in a bank, and we were all in cubes. I collaborated closely with a co-worker on the same project. We had disagreements, but I simultaneously tried to work things out with him as we sat so close to each other all day, I didn't want the conflict. Collaborative anger has you willing to retreat to maintain a longer relationship. This was also a bit passive-aggressive, but it meant we could tolerate our proximity and sanity with each other.

INDIRECT CONTROL

This is when someone is still trying to control the environment when they're angry during a conflict situation. On the outside, it may seem collaborative, but their objective is forceful. They have their agenda which they are pushing. So, they can also be manipulative. They can prevent the situation from escalating out of control using forceful methodology.

Again, with this strategy, you can win the war, but you are going to have casualties along the way. This type of anger control is best used when the person involved is not a close co-worker or has a common bond with you.

So, this could be an incident at a mall or in a store and you must institute a conflict de-escalation.

It's a completely different situation when you are a co-worker at a business, or in a relationship, and there's no familiarity with the person that is involved. The indirect control method is like being a police officer and you have a domestic incident where people are intoxicated and someone, or a group, must leave the premises to defuse the situation.

It may seem that the de-escalator is helping solve the situation but all they're doing is to get whoever needs to leave, to go. So then, some air can be let out of the balloon and the situation can be controlled, not trying to get to the bottom of whose fault it was but by letting air out of the person's balloon, so it doesn't burst.

Do you see yourself in any of these situations when you work around anger? I'm sure that you've been in one or more of them. I've been in all these situations, and sometimes a mix of them. This can get very complicated as you veer from one kind of situation and type to another. If you're well versed in these four things around anger it will stand you in good stead.

RADICAL REACHING OUT

Caring and sharing is an overused clichéd statement. It is also very misunderstood. People use this phrase at the drop of a hat, is never followed through and becomes meaningless. Proper caring and sharing can deconstruct a deadlock and allow the way forward without any roadblocks. However, when it comes to anger, would you feel it would be impossible to go for any reconciliation?

It figures, though, that this would be the best time to try it out. It could take people by surprise, and they would be so astounded they would agree to your offer. This is radical, though. Alternatively, they could reject it with the same fervor and leave you humiliated. People are generally terrified of rejection so would normally not go for the reconciliation method. It's a shame because I've seen it used to profound effect in crisis de-escalation. You have to gather your courage and then aim it squarely at whomever you are going to approach.

I've seen anger turn to calm in the blink of an eye and be so amazed I thought I was seeing things. Not only that but what followed was just as amazing. The person who was like a bull in a China shop agreed to a discussion! In this post-apocalyptic situation where the reverberations from the anger were still being felt around the room, it was like the heavens had deposited bucketloads of serenity. It was like Mozart himself stepped in to play.

Right, before you try this radical approach, ensure you know what you want to say, try it out quickly in your head, add the comma and hyphen and go for it. Note: The angry person must be sober. If there's alcohol involved, leave it well alone. It's a trigger-word situation.

One word could do the trick. All the previous rules of de-escalation are still firmly in place. The only thing we have added here is the first technique – going for it with all the force of the anger but using the power of positivity and healthy energy available to us with astounding effect. This "active constructive" reaching out has been researched in the US and has been used in controlled situations to profound effect. I have only seen it used twice, both with staggering results. It is most definitely not widely used for the very reason that I have stated above – fear of rejection.

Should de-escalators fear rejection? No, they shouldn't, but at the same time, this methodology takes a load of practice. If you go into this incorrectly, it could escalate the situation you are trying to defuse. And you could be rewarded with a slap or punch. All in the line of duty,

I'm afraid. Used correctly, it is a breakthrough in anger management.

It has been demonstrated by the research that the people succeeding with this method are normally leaders that would do well on the battlefield. In other words, today's business environment. Or de-escalators at the top of their field. Non-fearing but careful and astute. It's the kind of person who thinks very quickly and has summed up the situation in a couple of seconds that does really well.

The saying "think on your feet" takes a new dimension here. And it's something we de-escalators should be doing a lot more of.

Recap: Knowing the types of anger and how to deal with them is an integral part of a de-escalator's job. Conflict resolution is normally all about anger and how to defuse it. There are tried and tested methods that will see you win through in volatile situations if you stick to the game plan. Know these methods backwards and role-play them with coworkers so you will not be taken off guard.

STRATEGY THREE - MANAGE THE ANGER

#Crisis #Trigger #Escalation #Breaking Point #Recovery #Deflate Balloon

Understanding the cycle around anger is pivotal to your success in conflict de-escalation. There are four stages in this cycle.

Stage One - an incident or event trigger.
Stage Two - the escalation of emotions.
Stage Three - the breaking point – the catalyst for resolution.
Stage Four - the recovery.

Most of us have been in a crisis at some time in our lives. It could be a loss of a family member, loss of a job, loss of a house or a custody battle. Life can indeed be trying at the best of times.

It could be a combination of many small things that become overwhelming. There's just so much that can lead someone into a crisis. How it usually rears its head is with a stressful situation and loss of emotional control.

How did we manage those crises? What do we feel on reflection of those times? What was our behavior like? What did we say to people? Did we behave badly? Do you wish that you could change the way that you reacted? What did you say?

If you're reading this, you can look carefully at those situations while plotting to improve your skills in conflict de-escalation. If you had the tools that will be detailed in this book, could you have managed the situations very differently?

I can answer that easily in the affirmative. Once you have those all in your toolbox so to speak, you will conduct yourself in a way that will become astute in conflict resolution. For the person prone to such trigger motivation, explosive events could be a daily occurrence. The person is unstable and anything can begin the cycle.

Their reality is in that moment is something different to what you and I perceive. It is fraught with violent possibilities, even if it is momentary. Especially if it's momentary. It seems to happen with the most disparate bunch of people – the Sunday School piano player at the church, or the insurance salesperson. Or the math teacher that we are all fond of.

This is what makes this so dangerous. It is unexpected. You're caught off guard, so you're vulnerable. While at the same time as you can't live your life waiting for these events to happen, you can teach yourself, a little bit of yourself, to be always aware and expectant even among the most laid-back people, that anything is possible.

HIGH JINKS WITH MY SON

I'm going to give you an example of my 9-year-old son. Yes, my son. Children can present you with some great examples of conflict de-escalation possibilities. Every parent is very aware of the difficulties in raising children! My son, like sons everywhere, is an avid video gamer. Anyway, my son loves to play John Madden football on the Xbox. When he's being rude, argumentative, and disobedient, one of his privileges, the Xbox, gets taken away.

One day, when he was being truly 'otherwise,' I took his Xbox away, together with the controllers, so there was no way he could play his game. For him, this was a trigger and he started to go through the stages of anger. The second stage of anger is an escalation of emotions. Here, the person will visually or verbally express discomfort and frustration. There is normally an increased heart rate, the body tenses, and the voice changes tone.

My son's voice started to go higher, and his body was so tense it was almost rigid. We quickly processed what was happening. The escalation of emotions was when the voice started to change, the body became rigid, and his face went red. He then moved on to the third stage, which is the breaking point. The person is like a balloon full of air, and this is about to pop. You have to try and get some air out of the balloon.

Remember, you're not trying to find the underlying cause of what happened or whose fault it is (in his reality) when someone is at breaking point. There is little chance of any sense or logic at this stage. Anger has overridden everything. And for him, it is the total injustice of it all. You don't need to know the color of the balloon, who blew the balloon up, how it got so big or whose fault it was.

Do not go down any of these routes. You just need to get air out of the balloon, just enough so that it doesn't burst. Don't forget at this moment, the person has impaired reasoning and judgment. They have reduced capacity to hear what you are saying. The words will not be understood at all. The mind is fixated and obsessed with the trigger event. That is the total reality at this stage.

This person may start acting out. They may yell and start making threats. They may become more argumentative. They could even get violent. They are totally out of control. Can a 9-year-old get like this? Oh yes. I'm sure you know all about it, but how you manage it is vital. Now and for their future.

For a child, these emotions are completely overbearing. It's almost like if action is not taken, he will implode. My son was yelling at me. His shouts were so loud you could have heard him at the mall down the road. He then bolted up the stairs, and fled into his room, slamming the door. I had to let air out of the balloon! He was already at the breaking point stage.

How could I bring him down, let some air out of the balloon so it didn't burst? How to get him to stage 4, the recovery stage, and fast? I just left him alone. I did not rush after him, yelling just as he had done to me. Many people make the mistake of doing this. They get as angry as the child and, of course, that situation can end disastrously. Some 20 minutes later, my son came down the stairs bashfully. He was in stage 4, the recovery stage.

In this stage, when the adrenaline starts to normalize, the person can start hearing normally and thinking rationally, and they become more aware of what just happened. Often this is followed by guilt and shame and even remorse. Time to reflect had worked wonders. A crisis is a moment in time. It comes and goes. A person cannot live perpetually in such a state.

Sometimes, wait for it to go. My son had realized that he had gone too far. A solution or resolution to the issue that had escalated had to be found. I mean, how could a video game morph into a life-and-death situation? To an adult, of course, this would be ridiculous. To a child, not so. That video game represents his reality at that time, and it was a reality that had been endangered.

For him, it was a fight-and-flee response. When he came down the stairs, his head was down, and he wasn't making eye contact. He felt embarrassed. The crisis was over. I was calm, working on my computer. I glanced at him and silently continued working. It was time for him to make some positive choices.

What are the things that you can do? There's a great TV series you have recorded. Ask him if he would like to watch it with you. You could play a game together as a family. These are positive choices that are the exact opposite of what just occurred. It puts his behavior into stark relief. He knows this immediately.

So, in this recovery stage, the person (my son) starts to reflect on how badly he behaved and that he had overstepped the mark. However, he was not going to apologize. His body language, though, was his apology. With his head down, not making eye contact, illustrated he was embarrassed and remorseful. That's enough.

DON'T demand people apologize. This is often the case. The mother or father waits, furiously, for the errant son to appear and then let him have it. Very wrong. With his attitude, he is saying he's sorry. You don't want the crisis to continue. Your son will hopefully, with your correct behavior, become a well-adjusted person.

He's going to have tantrums. Any child or teen that didn't I would say was a bit peculiar. Let them rather have those tantrums now than at 26. If you go at the child continuously, he's going to hold a grudge which could grow into something explosive. Don't break your child's spirit.

I was probably the most proactive that I have ever been. My silence spoke volumes. It is the hardest thing you are ever going to do. It is a natural human reaction to fight back, to be judgmental, to retort in the same kind of language that has been aimed at you. Don't do it. Stop. Breathe. Think of the best time of your life. Let that feeling wash over you. Let the love for your child or the person fill your mind.

I'm not saying you should go overboard and start dancing around with your hands in the air. Your son could take this as a sign that you couldn't care, and even though he's not going to get to use the Xbox for a while, he may think his attitude hasn't bothered you much. It's a delicate balance. Use my example. It works. It's very hard, but hey, you cannot expect it to be sunshine all the way, or even some of the way, but it's the best way.

KICKBOXING FIGHT OVER A BROKEN LIGHT?

This boxing champ was prepared to do battle over a broken brake light.

Andre McIntyre was, at one point, the World Thai boxing champion and British Kickboxing champion. At the end of his career, his life unraveled into drugs and regular arrests followed. I was working as a young police officer at Reading Police station in the UK. Andre was living in Reading, which is close to London.

Due to his background in martial arts, he seemed to enjoy toying with the police and was well known to the station staffers in Reading. One summer night around 3am, I was patrolling alone when I saw a car with a rear brake light out.

So, I stopped the car and found it was being driven by McIntyre. He got out and immediately started bouncing on his toes like he was about to "roundhouse" me. I knew that I was at a disadvantage in skill and size, so I was faced with a difficult situation. However, I remembered that saying in conflict de-escalation "This isn't about me this is about him."

He was about to escalate the situation far greater than it needed. I mean it was just that his brake light was out, and he was bouncing like he was about to roundhouse a police officer and do who knows what. I very calmly told him that I had stopped him to say that his light was out and when he had the opportunity, to go and get it fixed in the morning. I turned to go back and got into my car.

I caught a glimpse of him standing there, his hands ready like he was in a kickboxing fight but frozen to the spot, shocked by what I had said to him. He had expected an escalation and was shocked when the exact opposite happened. I didn't lose, I didn't compromise, even though he had got out of his car looking for trouble. I wasn't going to allow that to happen.

The nature of the crime didn't warrant anyone getting hurt, him doing something he would regret and being arrested and going to prison for assaulting a police officer. So, the incident was de-escalated. I downplayed the situation and gave the same response I would have given to anyone - go and get it fixed!

As I got in my car and drove away, I could still see he was outside his car shocked as to what had happened. He was so sure that violence would occur and was dumbstruck when it didn't, so his actions were immediately de-escalated.

Recap: Know the stages of anger thoroughly. They must become so much a part of you that you really don't have to think about it anymore. If you don't know them off-pat, while you're thinking about what is happening in a volatile situation, everything could change for the worse.

STRATEGY FOUR - FIND THE VOICE OF REASON

#Value Dominant #Impairment #Logic Dominant #Intoxicated #Training #Escalation #Destraction #Rapport Builder #Proactive #Effective Listening

The story so far:

You've been taken on a journey of de-escalation, the stages of a crisis, and different styles of anger. This is becoming a very genuine experience for you and your aching to get into training so you can start playing a pivotal role in de-escalation too.

DETERMINING THE PERSONALITY TYPE

The two main personality types are value dominant (emotional) and logic dominant. If you're called to a de-escalation, you'll soon be able to figure out what type of personality they are and tailor your response accordingly. The voice of reason goes beyond that, though, if you're dealing with cognitive impairment from substance abuse. This does not pick a personality – it could be either value or logic dominant. How these people react when intoxicated can be a great test for you.

Have you ever tried to reason with someone who was intoxicated? You know how frustrating and futile it can be. Most of us who are sober have tried to de-escalate someone who is substance abuse impaired. They are not going to be responsive to any questions asked of them. And so, this is the question here, will you find a voice of reason within the person so you can de-escalate the situation?

However, this does not mean we should give up entirely on our mission. Naturally, we should grab the first chance to talk to them when they are sober. This will entail taking them home (if they're somewhere else) and coming back when they are cognitively more receptive and responsive.

There are occasions that require an immediate response. We must ask ourselves, where is that voice of reason which is powerful enough to ignite a spark in the impaired mind, allowing clarity, however briefly, to allow us to find the rational person and de-escalate? This is possible, and it requires thorough training to find any success. In this situation, focus on the present, and keep your sentences short.

Where, in a 'sober situation' you would be asking all sorts of questions, long and short, complex, and simple, here you must pick words that should resonate in the impaired mind. Naturally, this also depends on the stage of intoxication. If the person is on the verge of losing consciousness, your mission would be futile. Hopefully, there is still some cognitive ability to hear the voice of reason.

This really means is there even a possibility in talking the person down from their heightened state or intoxication. So, assuming reason is possible, the sentences must be short and pertinent. No beating about the bush here. A limited attention span requires pertinence and simplicity of the highest order.

Here's a great story which happened shortly before I engaged in training a company in de-escalation. It was a very unsettling situation for this company, and they needed the arsenal to know how to deal with such a traumatic experience should it happen again.

Some time back, I collaborated with a major company on de-escalation. They called me and said we really need training on how to de-escalate people who are in crisis or in highly charged situations. They were a large manufacturing company, one of the biggest in the US and one of the hubs is in Minnesota, where I live. I always ask before I start training, what's the primary reason for me coming? – what triggered this move?

They explained to me that there had been an issue with an employee's performance, and he had been spoken to several times by HR. Finally, he needed corrective action and this person ended up being terminated. Afterwards, he gained entrance into the building and had put the VP in a very compromising position. I can't recall everything that had happened… what wasn't known is that the employee's family relied totally on that man's position. It was up to him to support them. His work meant everything to that family.

When he lost his job, he was then fighting for the survival of his whole family. He went into a very highly charged emotional state, wondering how they were going to survive. With the employee's life in crisis, he didn't know what else to do other than to go back and fight and plead for his job.

He didn't know how he was going to pay the bills; the house was going to be foreclosed, he couldn't make his car payments, and how was he going to put food on the table? The only thing he could do was to go back and plead for his job.

Now, here's the interesting thing. The employee returned to work, entering by a door that was open because a current employee was going out. The employees had not been told of this high-risk termination, so another employee had held the door open for him. This move had led to the ensuing confrontation. Lesson learned - when doing a high-risk termination make sure all ground is covered and other employees know of the termination.

The employee who had been fired didn't return alone, now with his mind full of worry, confusion, anger, pain, and his life completely in crisis. He returned to work with his three young children all under the age of 8 and headed straight to the office of the VP of Operations, as he felt this person was to blame for his termination.

He walked into his office with his three kids to find the VP typing away on his computer. He shouted at the VP: "LOOK WHAT YOU DID." The VP looked up in shock and fear…he was concerned for his safety and didn't know what this man was going to do as he was highly charged and emotional. Someone who was in the know walked past the office, saw what was happening and alerted security. Meanwhile, the VP had been talking as calmly as he could, trying to find the voice of reason with this man. The VP kept on wondering how this man had gained access to the building.

There were important lessons learned by the company and they wanted to ensure that the correct procedures and training were put in place so it could never occur again. Hence the reason for them wanting to see me. They needed training, as do most companies employing staff members.

The fact that the VP was unhurt was amazing. Instinctively, he had used the tools of active listening, paraphrasing, and nodding, and giving the man an opportunity to be heard to demonstrate to him that he was taking him seriously and lastly gave him positive choices.

Refer to the story right at the beginning of the book (strategy 1) where we found a lady in an emotional crisis. Keep in mind how that situation was managed. Another situation could involve a father who has had a non-contact order placed on him regarding his son. He hasn't seen his son in six months. He goes to the preschool to see his son, but he is barred by the school from doing so because of the non-contact order. He has been told he's not allowed to be within 300 feet of his son.

So, you're talking to him soon after an explosive reaction from him at the school. Now, he's naturally in a highly charged state, and very emotional. Will you find the voice of reason to manage this situation successfully? De-escalation is called for, but in his reality, there must be an element of trust and understanding that he will relate to. In his reality, everyone is against him. We don't know the background of why a court order has been placed on him.

So, we must let some air out of his balloon to rationalize the situation. His thinking will be all over the place. If we can neutralize the force of negativity, then we have a gap and use that window to find the voice of reason. Again, this takes training and timing. You must figure out how long that window is going to stay open for you to be able to de-escalate.

You must be intuitive. Big time. Know reactions, be pre-emptive, so you can go for the gap when it opens itself to you. Be careful of what you say and don't offer to change his reality. Just offer some stability and reason for that moment. If you can follow up, do so at a moment which is less toxic. Then the voice of reason will be far more audible, more trustworthy, and more understanding. Remember the voice of reason is about finding your opportunity for them to see logic.

This requires a lot of learning and understanding on your part. Is someone value dominant (emotional- right brain) or logic dominant (left brain)? Determining what they are will go a long way in figuring out how to manage a de-escalation situation.

It is my understanding that, people don't put enough emphasis on personality types. They could have far more successful interventions if they did. Let me, at the outset, give you a simple demonstration of the types.

My eldest son is value dominant. When he has tasks to do around the house I say, "well done" and "that's great," "you did a wonderful job and I'm proud of you." He works on the values of being affirmed that he's doing well. My younger son is logic dominant. I ask him to clean his room and pack his bag for soccer practice, get his snack and drink as well, and he does everything I asked him to do. When I ask him if it's all done, he replies in the affirmative, I say "well done, thank you, you did an excellent job," he looks puzzled. "I did exactly what you asked. Why are you thanking me?"

The two types of people are quite different. My value son waits for confirmation and affirmation. My logic son just wants to get to the soccer field. In an adult de-escalation situation, you won't know what type a person is until you've started talking to them. Knowing that, it is helpful when it comes to de-escalation. You'll know what triggers them; you'll know what questions to ask and how to respond to their questions as well.

In conflict situations, which are charged and volatile, in the height of anger, there are conversations like "you said my mother does that" "I never did" "Yes you did" "When?" "The other day. Six months ago," "I like your mother" "No, you don't, and I don't like yours" and so on. One of your typical domestics, and there are so many of them. Once you've managed as many of these de-escalations as I have, you become astute in personality types and how to figure them out as quickly as you can and how to manage the situation.

When I was a uniformed police officer, arguments between two people were a common source of conflict that needed de-escalation. Aggression, physically and verbally, towards us came rapidly after our arrival on the scene. We would be bombarded with stuff like "You're just a cop. You're so young, what do know about anything? These situations can get out of control with the two opponents, and abuse rears its ugly head.

Can you change this situation? Can you find the voice of reason? If you have spotted the personality types, which is quite difficult in these situations, then you stand a chance as you will know how to approach the de-escalation. You must become shrewd in working it out quickly. You must think on your feet and move when the info you've been looking for comes to you.

We'll be getting onto the techniques you must use in another chapter, but this conundrum of differentiating personalities is basic and important. It could mean success or failure. If someone has deflected their anger from their opponent and onto you, how will you respond? Do you return a punch, or do you step aside? Leave the situation and let someone else step in? We are now going to explore:

> # How to find the voice of reason by knowing the personality types.
> # How to make informed, reasoned decisions with knowing value and logical types of thinking and responding.

HABITS OF LOGIC-DOMINANT PEOPLE

They pay attention. They will give you their full attention. For them, the answer lies in the detail, and they will scrutinize details thoroughly, even if they know them by heart to ensure every "T" has been crossed and 'i' dotted. In an argument, they need to know when, where, what time, what day, every detail is important. If the other person gets it wrong, the conflict is likely to escalate. If the other person is also logic dominant, you'll have an exasperating fight on your hands as to what happened at what time. They will be obsessed about this. They normally will trade blows at the drop of a hat, especially if any bit of the detail is, to them, not correct.

They will try to the utmost of their ability to ensure the validity of an accusation. If it fits with what they believe to be correct, then it's a fair fight. They would even be willing (maybe) to concede. If it's an unfair fight, anything goes. Hands, boots, garbage cans, whatever. They will fight to defend the right of something.

They will reiterate the clarity of their agenda, which will fit with what they see is objective and truly clear. A detailed and correct perception is what they hold dear and if pushed, will defend that at all costs.

Being logical, their objectives are sound and will stand the test of certainty. It's like if the take-off speed is Y, and the distance is X, then it follows that time taken will be YX. It can't be disputed, That's that. In an argument, another logic value person could be stubborn, knowing their opponent is correct, but wanting to get the better of them anyway.

If they come up with a plan, or what they believe to be a good idea, it needs to be validated against its origin, so it's a proven dynamic. It's not merely a good idea. It's a fact. Facts are good. Airy-fairy ideas are not. When confronted with suspicion or confrontation, they will insist on the facts. If their plan has been in any way been dismissed for any reason, a fight will ensue if there are no facts to back the other's argument.

They never assume anything. Assumption is the art of failure is a common saying among logic-dominant people. They say: explain clearly in words of true reflection and effect, and you will have conveyed correctly. The true meaning of something is only accurate and compelling if it's displayed with passion and truth.

There is nothing unclear or insincere about their language or habits. Clear precision is what they like best. Ambiguous language or behavior does not fit well in their dossier. There is nothing unsure about them. You will know where you stand and what they stand for. Mixed feelings are for others, but certainly not for them.

They believe strongly in the saying "The truth will set you free." Not necessarily on religious grounds, but on practical terms. If you are promoting untruths, you are likely to land up ingloriously in a soggy pit, according to them. With the logic dominant, be careful what you say. If it is an untruth, it is likely to be discarded without fear or favor.

HABITS OF VALUE-DOMINANT PEOPLE

On the opposing side, value-dominant people have a completely different agenda. Value-dominant people talk about "feeling." The logical person will say: "Come here. There's no way you will not understand how good this is going to be for you." The value-dominant person will reply "You don't understand. You have no idea how I feel about this. I won't do it" It is unlikely that this mix of personality types will ever see eye-to-eye unless there is a willingness to morph into that type to avoid arguments. Many a crisis will evolve from this partnership.

Value-dominant people will have an acute sense of justice because of the emotional ties that bind them. Emotions are very fluid, so you could find the value dominant person at odds with anyone making them feel uneasy because of their feelings of acute injustice. Or so it may appear.

A logic person will demonstrate how the angle of the rocket makes re-entry to earth safely and will even draw equations for you. However, the value dominant would have been lost long ago, wondering at the beauty of the clouds, and thinking how you would be feeling being in the rocket at that time.

The value-dominant person will seek affirmation at every corner and will be completely thrown if this is not given. If praise is not forthcoming, they could well not feel included. It's not that the overseer person didn't think it praiseworthy, they just forgot to do it, also not thinking it was that vital. In the workplace, many a de-escalation takes place around this issue.

Empathy is critical. They relate to others and their situations, which are often not ideal. Empathy is handed out to anyone that the value dominant person wishes to give it to. They will go out of their way to empathize strongly with people they deem to be in need, even after a bad incident. Some people will always take advantage of those seeking to do good and this could end disastrously.

Leading on from empathy is gratitude. They are thankful for many things that a logic-dominant person wouldn't even think about. Just watching the war in Ukraine, which is raging at the time of writing, they find themselves in an emotional meltdown. The logic-dominant person would be thinking if only the Ukraine army had concentrated on XYZ, this incident may have been avoided.

Contrary to popular opinion, value-dominant people can hold their own in crisis situations. They would not go out of their way to start one, but once in it, they can be strong and hold off attacks in a passive-aggressive kind of way, which tends to throw logic-dominant people for a loop. They can adapt easily to various situations, depending on what they are. If they feel threatened in any way, they will get out of the situation they are in. If they are in pleasant places they become easily contented.

Self-induced amnesia can be played with at will. This will happen when something particularly bad has happened in their lives, so they can forget about it and continue as if it never happened. They can slip in and out of this state to the extent they forget names, places, and dates. This state is rare, but it exists.

This type is very enthusiastic about accompanying people even to Alcoholics Anonymous or Narcotics Anonymous meetings for companionship. These are over-generalizations for both value-dominant and logic-dominant people. The point is that you get the gist of these personality types because you will meet them both in your de-escalation efforts.

"I'M GOING TO HURT PEOPLE TODAY"

When someone threatened violence at a church it took calm reasoning to halt the action in its tracks.

Wes Pederson is the Safety and Security Director of Eagle Brook Church Minnesota and is a good friend of mine and a good steward of all things regarding de-escalation. He shared this story with me. Eagle Brook Church is one of the largest churches in America with 11-plus campuses and 30,000 visitors per weekend.

During the annual indoor baptism, a gentleman that lives in the area, entered the church building and went straight to the café and ordered a small cup of coffee. He used a $100 bill to pay for his $2.00 cup of coffee and started to walk away. The volunteer that was at the cash register reminded him that he had change coming, but the man coldly stated: "I don't need it, I'm going to hurt someone today."

This startled the volunteer, so he wisely and immediately went to tell a staff member about what just happened. This reinforces the government's emphasis on "see something, say something." Very important!

One of our pastoral staff members, David, alerted our security team via radio and immediately called 911. I heard this radio communication and made my way to that area of the lobby. By the time I arrived, David was already talking with the man in the lobby. David asked the man if he would sit with him at one of the café tables and tell him about what was going on.

The man was very animated, and his angry voice carried throughout the lobby, causing others to leave the area. David noticed that the man was wearing a Notre Dame shirt, and commented on the shirt by asking: "Nice shirt, are you a Notre Dame fan?"

This seemed to result in the man temporarily relaxing a little. As the conversation went on, the man's anger escalated again. At this time, David went back to the topic of Notre Dame asking the man: "How are they doing this year?" He realized each time that he asked about Notre Dame it would result in a softened response from the man.

David continued to talk to him and asked, "What brought you here today?" The man's response was "I'm going to hurt people today." David said: "Why do you want to do that?" – to which the man replied, "I don't know" and his level of anger escalated again.

David asked the man if he had other Notre Dame items that he liked. The man said that he did, but they were at home, just down the road. David said "Man, I'd really like to see those items one day. But if you hurt someone, I don't think that will be possible."

After a five-minute conversation about Notre Dame, the man finally offered to go get the items to bring back and show David. When the man walked outside, one of our security team members discreetly followed him through the parking lot and motioned to the police who were now arriving, at the man's location. The police approached the man and had a conversation with him in the parking lot.

The man was once again escalating his anger as the police spoke with him. During the conversation, David was able to share with 911 dispatch that the man would de-escalate every time he brought up the topic of Notre Dame. This allowed the officers to do the same and eventually convince the man to voluntarily get into the ambulance so that they could get him the medical help that he needed. We later learned that this man was a war vet and was off his meds, which is what caused the delusions about wanting to hurt people.

KEY LEARNING

Some good things here. The volunteer did the right thing when the man said he was going to hurt someone. They didn't dismiss the comments as being a joke or allow them to rationalize what he said. Right away, they raised the alarm.

The second key thing that went well here is that the first person who saw the man and was so shaken by the threat that he intended to harm someone, immediately went in search of Pastor David, who approached the man to try and find intent. The intent is only found through questioning.

It started with some great distractions: removing the man from the area, taking him to the café, and using his Notre Dame shirt as a conversation starter and rapport builder. Changing his brain from right side (emotion) to left side logic, most of the questions that David asked him were logical questions which gave a better chance of making him think rationally.

Great listening skills from David and great awareness cues. They were smart enough to pick up on the cues that when he spoke about Notre Dame he would calm down. Great self-awareness and using what was around him to help defuse the situation and find out the intent of this man. Again, David used logic questions when he said he wanted to hurt someone. "Why would you want to do that?" he said.

Good example how being proactive (quick approach), using your body language, tone of voice, active listening and logic questions go a long way to de-escalating a person in crisis.

Recap: The importance of knowing the various traits of value-dominant and logic-dominant people cannot be emphasized highly enough. Once you

know the personalities of these various groups, your de-escalation could be made that much smoother. Also, the outcomes of your conflict resolution could be the difference between success and failure. If you are highly attuned to spotting personality traits, you will be able to determine the group within seconds.

STRATEGY FIVE - USE YOUR BODY AND VOICE

#Body Language #Non-Verbal #Active Listening #Cooperation #Tone of Voice #Being Bold #Supportive #Polite #Eager to Learn

How do you get the situation under control without having to make friends with the person or hand out ultimatums? It's called compliance. Co-operation takes skill, wisdom, and know-how. It can be difficult, for sure. It can be very difficult, depending on how explosive the situation is.

There is the use of your body language, tone of your voice, being intentional with the wording used and being consistent in your approach. Remember, too, conflict is not about you. It's about the person you're dealing with.

Let no ego come into your approach. If you do, it may intensify the situation and make it worse. The person you're dealing with is the one in crisis. Ego can also lead you to be judgmental, a big no-no for de-escalation. Body language and tone account for around 90% of our communication. How do we set ourselves up to talk to the person? Are we prepared to use the right words? Are we prepared to use no words at all? Sometimes, what we don't say speaks volumes.

This quote from Will Durant is pertinent here – "To say nothing, especially when speaking, is half the art of diplomacy." Sometimes, this is the most powerful form of communication.

Think of the times you've played Charades? That's the game where you can't use words, just actions, and people have to guess the answer. It can be difficult, but once you are proficient at de-escalation, you'll be a whizz around conflict.

When you are trying to de-escalate, the first item to make an impact on a person's behavior is your body language. You may or may not be aware of your own body language, but how you carry yourself can tell someone you are listening and open to suggestion, without a word.

If you're standing, you don't stand with your feet apart, legs stiff and arms folded. If you want someone to think you're an ex-military commander, this is the way to do it. Folded arms are a dead giveaway. That means you're closed to any outside input. Feet apart is aggression. You'll probably have a scowl, just to complete the picture.

You stand feet close to each other or one foot slightly more forward than the other. You can bend a knee. Arms are loose at the sides. Don't put your hands in your pockets. This can show you being disinterested.

Always respect personal space. We should all be used to this thanks to social distancing but in case you've forgotten, stand some 3 feet away. You are still in that person's space, but at least not right up against the face. If the person is ill at ease with you being so close, apologize and take a few steps back. Ask if that's okay. Always keep in mind what facial expressions and gestures you're using. Keep your face relaxed and calm. If you are told something unusual, don't react to it. You can nod your head.

Try and refrain from gestures that could be seen as threatening. Don't wave your arms about like the wind man outside a gas station. A great gesture is to make some points with an open hand close to your body. Sit opposite the person. Keep your hands on the table and open them when making points. Nod at salient points that the person is making. Smile, but not excessively. Don't drum your fingers on the table ever. This shows impatience, lack of courtesy and disinterest.

Speak at a normal pace, but don't enunciate like you're auditioning for a British play. Normal is the cue. Speaking of which, don't ever interject when the person is speaking. Wait for your turn. Don't put words in the person's mouth. Respect the person's feelings. He or she may be in a heightened state of anxiety, so your voice must de-escalate the situation. The point to learn here is that many people talk incredibly fast. This only creates more stress for the person trying to keep up. Slow it down but don't act condescending either.

Remember, if the person is stressed, they are not going to be paying too much attention to what you're saying, at first anyway. This is why your NVC – or non-verbal communication – is so important. They will take their cue from your behavior rather than your voice.

However, as things start to settle down, as they get to the voice of reason and start taking in logic they will switch to listening. Important, then, to keep your voice calm and behavior level correct as you begin your de-escalation. Regarding your talking, many, in a rush to get the negotiations over with, scramble to conclude the talking. Take time to listen and understand. Have you come to a perfect understanding of the situation and reached a comprehensible conclusion? In half an hour or an hour or so? Do you know how to plot a way forward for the person? Whatever you do, do not jump to conclusions!

All your training, all your "gut feel" would have been for nothing then. The eagerness for a quick fix will result in a sub-standard resolution. In fairness to you, but yet not a right to forgive the wrong, it could be that the conflict has produced so much anxiety for you, that you wish it to be over as quickly as possible.

But de-escalation can take time. Wisdom and experience play an important role in how the conversation moves along. If you have a partner, albeit not at the same level as you but maybe with an emotional quota that is greater, consider letting that partner take over for a while.

Go and sit in your vehicle. Relax and take some deep breaths. Do a quick meditation for five minutes – you have no idea what that can do for you. Right, you're ready to go back into the fray. Sum up quickly where your partner has led the proceedings to and start again. This mix-and-match has worked admirably for me and a less confident partner. Do the thing properly and methodically, no matter how long it takes.

A call-back, if that's possible, will have given you time to thoroughly explore the options of the proceedings and allow you to come to far better conclusions. Don't forget your voice is controlling all the above narrative. Any change in your voice through fatigue or anxiety will affect the person. Obviously, the situation would be completely different had it been a drug-crazed man with a gun. There's a whole new set of rules for that, including the priority, which is the police.

If the situation is safe, your words will respond accordingly, your manner of speech will respond and so too, your delivery. If it is a threatening situation, the scenario will adapt differently. If you were the first person to respond, you would call the police, or the police would have called you to accompany them.

Every situation demands a different response. As much as you would like to think so, every situation is not the same. Routines have to adapt. A particular circumstance will dictate how and when to conduct your delivery. Remember, conflict de-escalation is about concern for immediate safety. Physical harm in the here-and-now will be the primary concern and will dictate how you manage the situation.

In most situations, where harm is not evident, the field is open to your direct intent. Being intentional with your words can be the most salient point of the narrative. You can't afford to let one word go astray or have less meaning than you had intended. Every word, is, therefore, fraught with meaning, or rather, should be.

Even in these so-called peaceful negotiations, attitudes can change suddenly and without warning. You must be prepared for that. If it takes you by surprise, don't show it. Don't let your intent with prompt and meaningful wording collapse. Be prepared!

Your intent will change although your voice tone stays the same. Don't ever let shock and surprise get the better of you. You have nerves of steel. You're not a hero, but you're made of better things. You're a de-escalator. Fight-or-flight behavior patterns are most common in the interviewee. They could go from Mary Poppins to Cruella de Ville in five seconds. So, be stirred but not shaken. In other words, be prepared.

Don't forget, as a de-escalator, your intent is safety and fairness in all situations, and you are looking for compliance. Even though it could be that's the very last thing you care about right now because you're tired and anxious that this be resolved. You must overcome that and be the better self you strive for. Listen, you don't find great de-escalators by the busload. You won't find *any* de-escalators by the busload, even bad ones. You, however, are the best!

Go practice words with intentionality as per an evolving narrative over and over again. I've seen a de-escalator lose their cool after being insulted by the person being de-escalated. It's not personal. Remember, it's about them being in crisis, not you. Learn how to verbally react. Practice it until you're blue in the face, and don't get involved until you know exactly how to do this by heart. Watch every good hostage negotiator movie so much you long to see "The Sound of Music," which you loathe.

The saying "actions speak louder than words" is only partly true. Words can change a situation so completely that a trajectory springs up before you, showing immense promise for concluding this narrative, and you never even knew it was there. Well, you did, but you're just starting to figure out how to use your talent.

Don't go from Chris Rock the comedian to Frankenstein in one fell swoop. No, of course you wouldn't, except when you would. Just as much as you expect the unexpected from the interviewee, don't let the same be said of you. Nonverbal actions are often the culprit, and a situation could easily unravel. If you're not 100% committed to the task before you, you can have a serious lapse of judgment. Remember, remove all your distractions.

This lapse could see you become irritable, uneasy, thinking of where you would rather be, and horror upon horrors, rolling of the eyes. If that is caught by the person you are trying to de-escalate, you will either be targeted with verbal abuse or ignored completely for the rest of the de-escalation attempt.

Build on your skill and consistency talent and experience. Learn how to change the narrative with tone and body language without the conflict person even knowing it. This is to bring about meaningful change and pinpoint a route to a satisfactory de-escalation. If this is the first time you're doing this, you realize you could be taking a risk, but you know you're good, so you take it anyway.

It could go something like this:

DE-ESC: You said that it was due to this guy ... Kerr's actions that you decided to take matters in your own hands.

PERSON: I never said that.

[She did, but not in quite so many words.]

DE-ESC: (calmly) You said that Kerr was an instigator of (she looks at her notes) bad things.

PERSON: (slowly) He could sell you ice in winter. He knew how to twist you around. I hated him so much.

DE-ESC: But you loved him too.

PERSON: (getting agitated) He made me.

DE-ESC: (shivering, putting her arms around herself) Oh boy, I'm getting cold. Carl (she says to her partner) won't you fetch me a sweater, please?

Carl obliges.

PERSON: That's how he made me feel. Cold.

DE-ESC: Did you ever tell him that?

PERSON: (eyes blazing) Yes, I did. He threw me in a bath of cold water and said, "That's what makes you cold, not me!"

DE-ESC: That is seriously not a nice thing to do.

PERSON: Tell me about it. I hated him.

Carl brings DE-ESC her sweater and she slips it on.

DE-ESC: Oh, thanks Carl. This is so much better.

Person begins crying.

PERSON: That's what I wanted more than anything. To feel better, so….

DE -ESC: You packed your case and was going to leave.

Person nods, wiping away tears from her cheeks.

DE-ESC: So, you did take matters into your own hands. Good for you.

PERSON: Yeah. But then afterwards...

DE-ESC: Yup. We know he shoved you into a freezer.

PERSON: Not before I called 911.

This conversation was the result of DE-ESC managing to manipulate the situation for a resolution to take place with the person. This was not done in haste, but with eagerness. The DE-ESC hung onto the "ice" and "cold" words as the consistency triggers. The DE-ESC wasn't feeling cold at all, but she used the sweater as a means to an end. She happens to be a skilled de-escalator, especially when it comes to retaining consistency in approach. She knew "ICE" was a good trigger and that's why she went through the whole sweater thing.

There are also a number of words that were used that have the desired effect and are empathetic and act to affirm the person. The DE-ESC is always polite and eager to learn. She is supportive and builds compliance easily. Never does she condone anything or is judgmental in any way. This is how a DE-ESC should be with words. They are not there to be played with. They are there to build relationships and provide consistency and compliance. Inconsistency to me is one of my pet hates. In any situation.

For instance, I have a favorite restaurant here in America called Chipotle, where when I asked for a little extra portion, they would happily oblige, because I'm a regular customer. One day I attended and a new member of staff who didn't know me was serving. When I asked for extra rice, they said no. Next I asked for extra toppings and they said no. This inconsistency made me frustrated as they always said yes, but today it was a no!

Never be inconsistent in your approach, the lack of consistency can actually make the situation worse. It leads to uneasiness, disbelief, and irritation. Always consider this when trying to de-escalate a person. If your verbal approach leaps from one thing to the other, the person will have difficulty following you and will lose interest. That is no way to find compliance! I once went to a workplace where a manager was changing his views on certain things from one week to the next and his inconsistency was leading to frustration amongst their team.

This becomes an incident trigger, and that, as we know, is the first stage of the anger cycle. There was an enormous conflict in the workplace, especially between two of his staff. The thing is no one wanted this man to be fired because he really was very good at his job. He was just inconsistent at his work. This progressed to Stage

Two of anger, which is an escalation of emotions which rapidly led to Stage Three, breaking point and finally, to Stage Four, which was recovery. It must be remembered, though, that when people are in a heightened state of anxiety and frustration, sensibility can fly right out of the window. Remember, when you're a de-escalator, check your personal feelings and leave your ego at the front door. For good. Sometimes, you wonder how you will ever find compliance. It seems an impossible dream. Then, your work pays off and you suddenly realize it's here!

BEING BOLD IN FINDING COMPLIANCE

In 2011, I moved from London to Minneapolis. I had been to Minneapolis many times before, as a visitor, but this time was different. I was moving to the US permanently and was now searching for a job. I visited a career fair in downtown Minneapolis one day, and on my way home I stopped at a gas station to get a cool drink.

As I was going to the express shop, I didn't park at a pump, but a little way off. It wasn't very well-lighted as the only lighting was from the gas pumps, quite a way away. Out of habit, I ensured all doors were locked. (Essential!) Suddenly I saw two figures approach the car out of the dark, and then two more shortly after that.

All this happened in a few seconds. Now, there were four people standing around my car.

So, now, you know my police background, so my body and mind were very alert to some nasty possibilities. It's funny how that kicks in. I mean, obviously, anyone from whatever background would know what was about to happen, but someone from the police is already thinking about what to say, what to do. You didn't have to be a rocket scientist to know that very soon I could be at a disadvantage. I needed to de-escalate this situation. The conflict was looming.

Sometimes, in chronic crisis situations when you need to de-escalate a situation urgently, you need to be bold. If you feel that you're about to enter into a conflict, you can take the initiative. So here is what I did. I lowered the window, just enough that the man on the outside next to me couldn't get his hands in the car or open the door and drag me out. So, the conflict situation hadn't begun its active phase, but it was obvious it was going to. I used my voice only and ensured a quiet, calm tone.

In this calmness, I told them: "I am not going to be a victim. So go and find someone else to rob." He spoke for the first time and said they had no harmful intentions, and just wanted to see who I was. I naturally didn't believe that for a second. He was thrown because of my attitude, my words. I appeared as calm as a cucumber, even though I didn't feel like that. He never saw me as a threat.

What I did I don't advocate, but you may not have the means to do anything else. If you react differently to what I did – nervous, agitated, hostile, it could be used as a disadvantage to you and the men would have used that against me. If you have the time to get out of a hostile or volatile situation, even a slither of time that has been given to you, use it. Have the presence of mind to do that. In my case, I set the boundaries as to why I wouldn't be a victim. I de-escalated a situation before it got to the point of anger and conflict by using words that calmed the situation. The four men disappeared into the darkness.

I knew this would be a great teaching for someone on the rare occasion they would find themselves in such a situation. Make it clear, very calmly, that you will not be a victim, and you will not tolerate this hostile situation or their actions. You're going to put those boundaries in place. You will put the person standing menacingly close to you on the back foot. They are not prepared for positive assertion. You will have de-escalated a situation before it reaches the point of action.

Recap: The use of your voice and body language is vital in conflict de-escalation. Those are the only tools you have to use, so use them wisely. Build your

skill on talent and experience and watch the proceedings pan out smoothly. Always be ready, though, for the unexpected and however strange it may seem, prepare to roll with the dice. In other words, don't get thrown off course. Use your tools (voice and body) to the greatest effect. Practice, as they say, makes perfect.

STRATEGY SIX - ACTIVE LISTENING/DISTRACTION

#Active Listening #Listen to Understand #Paraphrase #Distraction #Right Brain #Left Brain #Honesty Wins #Empathy

Tried and tested ways of de-escalation have proven to be those that work. They have been honed to a fine art. We can't always predict human behavior, but we can say something has been perfected and is shown to be very effective. Behavior, though, will continue to throw the odd curved ball, which will need the de-escalator to go off script, yet remain within the confines of the rules of de-escalation.

ACTIVE LISTENING

In de-escalation, we must listen to understand, not to respond. You may think of all sorts of what you believe to be great words of wisdom, and you're being prompted to say them immediately, but refrain. Nothing beats listening! However, what we are going to give the person is minimal verbal encouragement and paraphrasing. This proves we are listening. We don't have to repeat word-for-word what we've heard. This is what paraphrasing is about. Just an acknowledgement that we are listening.

Active listening involves:

Making eye contact and facing the speaker

Face-to-face communication should include eye contact. However, making too much eye contact might be intimidating, so consider your surroundings. To demonstrate that you are paying attention, try breaking eye contact every five seconds or so. You may also alternate between looking at their eyes for five seconds at a time to demonstrate that you are listening. Gazing up or to the side as you look away is preferable to looking downward, which could imply that you wish to end the conversation. A little head tilt or resting your head on your palm can both indicate that you're paying attention.

Listening to non-verbal cues

You can learn just as much from a person's gestures, tone of voice, and facial expressions as you can from their spoken words. Consider what the other person is saying by their body language, such as whether they are grinning, defensively crossing their arms, or wiping their eyes to indicate fatigue or annoyance. Even when speaking over the phone, the other person's voice, which may sound mellow or enthusiastic, can reveal a lot about them.

Avoid interfering

Being interrupted annoys the other person because it conveys that you value your opinion above theirs or that you don't have time to listen to what they have to say. Force yourself to slow down if you naturally speak fast or think more quickly so that the other person can speak. Remember, you don't have to speak up if there is a gap or little period of silence. Allowing the other person to talk will also make it simpler for you to comprehend what they are trying to say. When the conversation diverts from what they were attempting to say, take the conversation back to "So, you were telling me about….."

Not reacting emotionally

It can be difficult to pay attention to what is said next if you begin to respond emotionally to what is being stated. Do your best to listen intently. Additionally, avoid supposing that you already know what will be stated after this.

Proving you're paying attention

To demonstrate that you're paying attention, nod your head, smile, and utter insignificant noises like "yeah" and "uh huh." Avoid fidgeting, checking your watch etc.

Never forcing your viewpoints or recommendations

Even though it's not always simple, listening to someone and offering support can be much more satisfying than giving them advice. Most people prefer to find their own solutions in all facets of life. If you must offer your excellent idea, first find out if they are interested in hearing it. For example, you may ask, "Would you like to hear my suggestions?"

Posing inquiries

By politely and thoughtfully clarifying what has been stated, you can demonstrate that you have been paying attention. When in doubt about your comprehension, wait until the speaker takes a pause before asking, "Did you mean that?" Alternatively, "I'm not sure if I got what you were saying about..." Additionally, wherever possible, utilize open-ended inquiries like, "How did it make you feel?"

This all has a remarkable, uplifting effect. It confirms that we understand how they are feeling. It doesn't mean you agree with what is being said. It proves you are listening! I think it's fair to say guys have more of a problem with active listening than women, but once you attune yourself to it, it's not as difficult as you think. It's such an important part of de-escalation, you really must get used to it.

This is a way of repositioning the conversation away from the crisis or conflict. When I was a police officer, I used to get called to domestic arguments. My partner would stay inside and talk to one of the crisis partners and I would ask the other one to go outside with me. This wasn't purely to avoid a balloon full of air popping with both parties present, although that was very much in mind, but also to cause a distraction from the situation.

There are times when "out of sight is out of mind" can be valid, and this is one such instance. If one of the persons can't see the other, there will be less distraction in trying to find the voice of reason and more focus on talking and listening to increase the chances of de-escalation. As an example, when my sons argue over something, I remove one of them and my wife stays with the other. We give our sons something fun to do on their own, and the argument is rapidly forgotten.

What we are attempting, and I spoke about this earlier, is to navigate between left brain-right brain hemispheres, or the logic versus the value dominants. When we are distracting someone, we try to move brain modes and appeal to the one that is lying dormant. Things are then seen from a different perspective, and so the situation is defused. The left side focuses on logic, language and numbers and the right side on imagination, color, and emotion.

For instance, last year I was looking to buy a home for my mother back in England with my brother as where my mum was living was not ideal for her. My sister became concerned that my brother and I were not moving fast enough and would lose a great deal on a house we liked. My sister's decisions were focused on the right side of the brain thinking that my mother might not be cared for, safe and happy. And I had to get her to move over to the left and start thinking logically about the home. It had to be the right house in the right location at the right price.

While it may have appealed to the emotions, it would be the logic side that sorted it all out. Everything about a house sale needs logic – is it a good deal? Is it a good investment? Does it need renovations and, if so, how much will that cost? When you're trying to distract someone in the de-escalation process, you work in the same way by shifting between logic and value dominants. This could be a simple question like "How many people did you notice when you walked in?" If the person was in an emotional state (value dominant) then this question begins to move them to the left. This is a great distraction tactic.

Recap: Switching from left brain to right brain in a de-escalation might prove the only way to go, so learn how to do this seamlessly. Also, active listening techniques are the method that has proved time and again to be the correct way of de-escalation. Ensure that you know these techniques thoroughly.

STRATEGY SEVEN - FOSTER GOOD CONVERSATIONS

#Being Totally Sincere #Paraphrasing #Careful Questions #Willingness #like to Learn More #No Closed-Ended Questions #Calm Persuasive #Need Full Story #Empathy Not Sympathy #I Versus You

In 2006 the British Security Services were receiving intelligence of terrorists planning to kill hundreds, if not thousands of people with a plot to smuggle liquids on planes, make the bomb on board and then blow the planes up. As the security services are intelligence focused and do not prosecute, they shared the intelligence of the bomb plot with police so that the danger could be averted.

The case is known internationally as the "liquid bomb terrorism plot" and it's the reason that to this day you cannot take more than 100ml of liquids on airplanes. At the time, I was working in our organized crime division in the British police, using covert police tactics like phone taps, surveillance, listening devices – all the exciting stuff you see on TV. We were asked by the British Security Services to get an observation post of one of the terror suspects homes so that they could be monitored. Two detectives were sent out for this task but came back empty-handed.

My partner, Sally, and I were then sent out on the same mission. We had better luck. After being out for 20 minutes in the street where the suspect lived, we found a good observation post with a great view of the suspect's residence, in a home of a 20 something guy who was more than happy to do his civic duty in fighting the war on terror.

One of the requirements by the security services was to tell the owner of the house we would be using it for "A matter of great national security", which, as you can imagine, would put many people off helping and get a "sorry would love to help but…" type of response. This young resident was proud as anything to be doing this for us and his country, why? Because of how we communicated the challenge to him.

There is a way to nurture a conversation to make sure you are successful. We had this in mind when talking to this guy. Your body language has got to be correct. What we were saying, how we were saying it has to inspire confidence in his safety. You must nurture the art of conversation and body language to build rapport.

I think back to the training I took from Chartered Forensic Psychologist Dr. Eric Shepherd, who taught the police some incredible tactics. He invented a program called Softens (Signs of Sincerity, Open Posture, Forward Lean, Touch, Eye Contact, Nods, Supportive Sounds). This is basically an expression of sincerity. He taught how to be totally sincere in voice and body. You can't fake this. You can try but I've known many who have lost a de-escalation because of this.

Their hearts weren't in it, and the person on the receiving end picked it up and made a de-escalation almost impossible. For instance, the "O" is an open posture. Your body language is going to express this. By leaning forward, you will show engagement and a complete willingness to learn and understand. You will show that you have been listening to everything that has been said.

You may lean in a little and touch the shoulder, which shows the person that you care about what's happening. What you are demonstrating is that "Hey, it's okay. We've got you here and we'll help." It's a gentle touch of communication. It's saying "You will come to no harm. We're here to support you." Just a word of warning – never physically touch any part of the other person's body except the shoulder. These days, you could find yourself on a harassment charge with the person reading your actions wrong.

Eye contact is very important. This shows that you're engaged. Don't make it a fixation. Taking some notes during this period is a good thing so you haven't got your focus on the other person all the time. They could get uncomfortable and agitated. Also, don't look at your notes to much as it could say your disinterested you must be present in the moment and find the balance.

Taking notes shows that you're still fully engaged. It's a delicate balance this exercise and it all comes together with practice. You're going to nod now and then, to show you've been listening. It doesn't necessarily mean you agree with what's being said. It shows you're being attentive.

Paraphrasing is also excellent, to show you're listening carefully and can repeat in small bites what has been said. When you nod the head, it shows that you understand what has been said. This is part of the Softens process, and it's one that completely changed the way that the police who were trained in this process, conducted questioning. For me, it was an excellent background for de-escalation. The procedure helped our complete approach. I use it all the time.

So, when dealing with someone who is in a highly charged state, you must know what verbal communication is necessary. What you don't want is a resistance to questioning. To lead a person down a path who is somewhat unwilling and very scared, takes a lot of practice and training on your part.

Dr. Shepherd is still active in the courts in Britain as one of the country's leading forensic psychologists. In simple terms, Dr. Shepherd describes his objective as 'trying to give the court an explanation of why a particular suspect, victim or witness would behave in a particular way'. Woe betides anyone who hasn't done their job properly, or who has missed certain cues and clues. He has garnered a striking reputation, installing fear and finesse into the court process. I owe a debt to Dr. Shepherd. He taught me things I will never forget.

So, we are going to garner facts by asking questions. Not in an interrogation style, but in a carefully worked out conversation style. Our questions will encourage the person to give information that will help in de-escalation of the situation. There are a number of simple ways of doing this. Start with the "WH" questions – who, what, where, when why and how? This will give you everything that you need to know. Urge the person to tell you what is happening right now. "Describe, if you will, what has happened to you that has upset your life. I know something happened at work. Tell me what happened?"

This shows an interest that you would like to learn more. It expresses that you need a better understanding of what and why the person is feeling upset. Another way of fostering good communications is by only asking singular questions. Do not ask multiple questions. This will distract and agitate. They don't know which one you want them to answer. So, make it one question at a time.

There will be many pauses. Go with the flow. Don't rush anything. "Tell me what happened today? What you say to us stays with us. How are you feeling about this? I can see it's causing a major distraction. If it's too much for you to handle, we can help." This is where you show active listening. You're going to nod, make supportive sounds, open hands, semi reach-out, paraphrase.

You're also going to avoid closed ended questions because we don't want "Yes" or "No" answers. They are very restrictive when you're trying to build rapport. We already have the basic information. We're looking to go behind the scenes as it were. "I understand that you're unhappy and from what we've heard you have every right to be. Tell me more so I can better understand?"

So, you are driving the conversation. Navigate those hairpin bends carefully. It's not a smooth road ahead. When someone is in crisis, give them the opportunity and space to deliver as much as possible. In their time. Don't force any issue and try and rush them as that's a big mistake. This is also where you slowly edge the situation from the right brain (emotional) to the left (logic), which will calm the person and uphold a rationale for a steadier deliverance. The only time that closed questions are needed is when you want to confirm facts. I reiterate, don't use multiple questions. This doesn't do any good to an already frazzled brain. We are trying to make them less confused and clearer.

How you ask questions is crucial however, don't be averse to asking questions that could be problematic. If they are essential for de-escalation, ask them. You may find there is a contradiction in the story. You have to clear this up, but at the same time you realize this could cause wobbles and a "You don't believe me!" accusation.

This is a difficult one, but must be asked, knowing you may have to start all over again if there are bits in the story that don't add up. There could be a logical reason for this because of the highly charged emotional state.

Let's face it, most of us have amended the facts now and then to make a story more believable and most times it is in jest. However, when you are in de-escalation mode, it's a different story, literally. If the person is lying to us, we have to pick up on this immediately.

Whatever you do, don't change your behavior. Remain calm and persuasive and gently try and reason why this has occurred. This could be the real reason for the conflict, and one that the person is trying to protect out of shame or bewilderment.

The human condition can be very puzzling, but nothing should throw us in our de-escalation. If you must build the conversation again, then that's what you do, being even more open and willing to listen. Urge the person to come clean with you in a gentle and unassuming manner. Tell the person that you understand. But also make it clear if you don't know the full story it will be very difficult to help, and that's your mission. You are there to help and re-direct people from emotional-intent to logic-intent and put them on a sound and even path.

You can usually spot the red flags in a story by their very convoluted nature. Often streams of the story will contradict what was said before. It could well be that the person does not want the truth revealed because it is humiliating. Don't try and pick holes in the story but glaring contradictions will need your attention. You will probably find the person to be far more open, honest, and relieved that the full story is being told, no matter how humiliating it could be.

This has happened to me on occasion, and normally after a gentle confrontation, the person exhibits a completely different persona. They are just relieved that they can get the problem off their chests, and they will unburden it all. It can be a very refreshing moment for the person you are talking to. Try and steer the conversation towards this path.

I have a story here inspired by Great Clips. Great Clips is an American chain of barber shops, and one that I visited when I first moved to the US. Every time I visited the shop, they would always ask the same question: "Welcome to Great Clips. What brings you here today?" So, I'm inside with my long Afro hair, and one would assume that it was obvious why I was there.

Anyway, they've asked the question, and I would reply: "I'm here to have my hair cut." And the barber says: "Great! We can help with that." As unassuming and nonsensical as this may be, it works. It makes you feel good.

Don't ever be afraid to ask someone who you are de-escalating simple questions such as the above. The great catchphrase KISS "Keep it Simple, Stupid" works every time. This can also start a conversation in the barbers, and normally does. The same situation could begin when you're with someone in crisis.

When someone is really agitated and angry you can say: "I can see you're really frustrated and angry. How can I help you with this?" State the obvious, like they did at Great Clips. You can't hide from the fact that someone is mad or agitated. Don't hide. That's why you're there.

A gentle confrontation is not easy. What is easy is also to be mad, which is the natural human reaction. However, always go for gentle persuasion with empathy. Ask questions that encourage a response. "So, are you here today to see someone?" is a closed question. Rather say: "What brings you here today?" Don't say: "Are you here to see Simon?" (closed) but rather "Who are you here to visit?" empowers the person to give you information. Don't ask a multiple question, like "Are you here for a visit? Or just looking around?" Rather say: "How can I direct you to a service today?" Again, you are empowering the person to provide you with information.

The next action to foster a good conversation is to use paraphrasing. Remember the story right at the beginning of the book about the woman who refused to leave the company after being terminated by HR? (*Strategy one)* I used paraphrasing in that conversation. It helped the person feel that she was being listened to and understood. A paraphrase should be kept short. When someone is in an agitated state, the ability to listen and process is dramatically reduced.

"Yes, you should have been told what time to report in, where to go and who to report to." You're going to paraphrase this and confirm the information so that there is no ambiguity, it tells the person that he or she is being heard and that they're understood. Now we're going to re-state statements to foster good communication.

You're working towards their goal, not yours. You're being collaborative and working to a common goal. We're, therefore, going to start using "We" "We need to work out a solution to this problem together so we can move forward today." Use positive and helpful statements like "I want to help you" and "Please tell me more so I can understand the situation better." "Let's call John. I know he would be able to help us with this." "Ms. Jones manages this for our district. Let's find out what she feels. She is always willing to help."

Once the person has moved over to the left logic side brain, you will be more able to successfully de-escalate more effectively. While the person is still in emotional territory, it is always difficult to negotiate anything.

Emotions are like a slippery eel. You can't grasp it fully and before you know it, will slide right out of your hands. Don't use pity statements like "Oh you poor thing." This may be an effort to show sympathy, but is, in fact, not very empathetic. It's putting up barriers and allowing the person to become more unhappy and does not aid rapport building.

Using Empathy, not sympathy

Here's the basics - sympathy is feeling compassion, pity, or sorrow for someone's condition. Empathy, on the other hand, puts you slap-bang in that person's shoes so you can understand why those feelings are present. So, you're not feeling sorry (as in sympathizing), you're understanding those emotions and developing kindness for that person.

Move consciously from left to right brain and focus your activities there. Here's a good example, remembering that in the human condition, we all make mistakes. Now, as a young police officer, I had to often give death messages to families. Once I had to tell a woman that her son had died, and she was in such shock she began to laugh uncontrollably.

Eventually, I sat down with her and told her the details. I made the rookie mistake of showing sympathy rather than empathy. It was like a car crash. As soon as the words came out – "I know how you must be feeling" instead of: "I'm really trying to understand how you feel." I remember it like it was yesterday. She gave me a look of disdain and said "How do you know how I'm feeling? How do you know what it's like?" Have you ever had someone say to you "How do you know how I'm feeling" or "How do you know what it's like"?

I felt like she really hated me at that moment, and I don't blame her. That's what happens when you replace empathy with sympathy. I never did that again. I remember a co-worker saying to me "When you're talking to someone in a highly charged state, they only catch a small percentage of your words. They're going to pick up on keywords and possibly use them against you. Which is what happened to me.

Silence is golden. However, it can be awkward if you're not used to working with this tactic. Learn to be comfortable with silence. It's also especially useful to demonstrate that you're listening intently. What's more, it gives you time to process what is happening. You could say: "It would be great if I could just collect my thoughts for a minute, and really try and understand what you've been telling me," Or "I would love to have a moment to reflect on what you've said so I can understand and process it."

Most times, silence can be deafening. People always try and fill silence up with something. They tend to find it very awkward. So, you ask a question and both of you are silent. Keep looking at the person. Do this long enough and the person will answer you. In fact, they will overshare and give you more and more information. The more you stay silent, the more they will try and fill that void. This can, then, be a terrific de-escalation tactic.

Use silence along with active listening to show you are really engaged. Use minimal prompts. Then, when they start sharing, they will start to remove the emotion stops, move to the logic stage, and start unravelling a bundle.

They put themselves in a paradoxical situation. By demonstrating silence, you are showing you are listening. You're truly hearing them. The longer you stay silent, the more they will feel heard. They will continue to speak, and you will let them as the more they unload, the better they'll feel and the more you know.

"I" versus "You" statements

"I-statements" reduce hostility and defensiveness and "you-statements" can provoke anger. Today it's a commonly accepted fact that the use of "I-statements" in relationships and even at work results in better communication. "You-statements" make the person feel that you are punishing them. When people feel attacked, they naturally become defensive. It's hard-wired into our DNA. By pointing out what they've done wrong, you're trying to make them change. Rather than inviting a productive response, you're inviting anger from the person. Not what you're trying to do! Don't use "you have to" statements like "you have to stop now" or "you have to quieten down." This will only escalate situations.

An "I-statement," on the other hand, shows you respect personal accountability. It can lower the tension of the moment, and saying you are not blaming him or her for your reaction. When using "I-statements," you display the openness for deep listening and resolution.

When you hear those dreaded words: "You always do this." "Why do you always do that?" As a husband and father, I've said this more often than I should, but we all make mistakes, right! The person this is aimed at will become defensive. If you use You-statements in a conflict situation, they are blaming statements and quite the incorrect way of going about things. You want to start using I-statements as quickly as you can. If not, you are going to build agitation and stress. Here are some of the most appropriate I-statements: "When you raise your voice, I feel agitated because I can't concentrate. I would like to hear a soft voice because that makes me think better." "I-feel statements" can help unearth real emotions, which the person has hidden, and they can start owning them. This is a wonderful way of empowering someone in crisis and letting air out of the balloon.

WHAT IT TOOK TO TACKLE "PROBLEM" KIDS

A public safety director provided a failed attempt at resolving a tense situation in school before someone with the correct de-escalation technique showed him how to do it properly.

Jim Larson had recently started a new job as a security officer of a high school. When taken on the tour of the school by the public safety leader, some kids in the school were identified as being "trouble" and kids to look out for. Jim saw two of the troublemakers in the school later that day and stopped to speak with them.

He found the two kids in good spirits, and they started calling him Jerry Garcia, joking that he looked like the American singer-songwriter Jerry Garcia, best known for being the lead guitarist and singer with the rock band Grateful Dead. Jim has a long beard which is clear white. "I think I look more like Santa Claus, but I see where the kids were coming from," he mused. Jim understands that when working around kids it's important not to take yourself too seriously and he was happy to partake in communication that made him part of the joke to build rapport with the kids. He said that when these kids left the school a few years later, they all brought in Jerry Garcia CDs for him to sign, as he said it became quite the running joke!

On Jim's second day, the public safety officer called to meet him outside a classroom as he needed to remove a disruptive kid. When Jim met up with the manager, he was told it was one of the kids identified to him from the prior day. He was being disruptive in the class, and he had to be removed to the principal's office.

The public safety manager said to Jim that he wanted him to have the experience of seeing how to remove a kid from the class so when he needed to do it, he would know what to expect. Jim said that the public safety manager entered the classroom while he waited outside.

There were around 30 kids inside the classroom with the teacher present. Jim said that from the body language demonstrated that it wasn't going well. He said both the kid and the safety manager were pointing fingers. Their stance looked defensive, and it was clear that the situation had become more escalated with the safety manager entering the room than de-escalating it.

Jim heard the kid shout: "Well then, go and get a police officer."

The public safety manager came outside the classroom and spoke with Jim. He quickly explained that the kid was rude and aggressive and was refusing to leave the classroom. He had said to him that if he didn't leave, he would call the police and the kid had said he could go ahead and call the police. The public safety manager said that he was now going to get the police.

Jim, who had met the disruptive kid only the day earlier and had started to build rapport with him after he had given him the nickname Jerry Garcia, Jim said: "Can I have a try?" The public safety manager said he could but doubted it would work. He reiterated they needed the police.

Jim said: "Let me try and then if he doesn't come out, we can call the police." So, Jim entered the classroom with the kids plus the teacher eagerly watching on. He approached the disruptive kid by introducing himself as Jerry which instantly started to break down the barrier.

He explained to the kid that he had to visit the principal's office for being disruptive and there was nothing he could do to change that. He said what he could change was how he got there. Reiterating that no one wanted him to leave the classroom escorted by a police officer. The kid said, "I'm not going to leave for that guy." Jim said: "Well, will you leave for me?" To which the kid said he would, packed up his stuff and left with Jim to the principal's office.

Later, when Jim and the public safety manager got together, he said that Jim had been soft and had compromised with the kid. It was obvious that the manager just didn't like being shown up. Jim learned that the safety manager's nickname was 'Robocop,' and he had a reputation as being stern and trying to muscle his way through every conflict situation.

Recap: Look at what is meant by "good conversations". They are the ones that lead to positive endings. You can create a template in your head and chose sentences from your memory bank that fit the situation. Examine the use of "I" and "You" in your sentences. Examine particularly the school situation story and the type of conversation that led to positive result immediately. Also, ensure you know the difference between empathy and sympathy.

STRATEGY EIGHT - REMOVE COMMUNICATION BARRIERS

#No Power Struggles #Dont Show Off #Understand Bias #Don't Judge #Don't Argue #Give Facts as Options #Use Cooperative Words #Don't Interrupt #No Clichés #Person Of Reason #Do Homework #It's Not Personal

Did you know that we put up the barriers that can influence the results of our de-escalation efforts? Yes, we do. So, let's see what we can do about that. It can have an enormous adverse effect, so the sooner we get to grips with that, the better. The barriers are things that we say and do. And we've done them sub-consciously, or even consciously!

How do we react against anger and confrontation? You'll come up with these forces many times in crisis situations. You may have these feelings within yourself and not be aware of it! We need to have an abundance of self-awareness when we react to hostility. Our subconscious behavior could make the situation worse, and we're not even aware of it. We should all remember that there has been a build-up of emotions often over a long time before being triggered from zero to 250.

You know the person who has to win at all costs? They cannot lose face by compromising with a person to resolve conflict. There is, however, often no winner or loser when resolving conflict. The person who feels they have to win makes de-escalation difficult. The person can sometimes not even be aware of their attitude.

A case in point is the story of the school where the public safety officer was winding the kid up when he was trying to remove the kid from the class. He thought this was de-escalation, but was, in fact, the exact opposite. We don't want to engage in a power struggle. When we confront this behavior and we are attempting to de-escalate someone in conflict, there doesn't have to be a winner and loser.

Something that the crisis person says could trigger something in you, and then the situation gets out of control. This will present itself as a nightmare to you and will always be there to remind you of what NOT to do. Remember "choices made in anger cannot be undone." This, then, will apply as much to you as the person you're trying to de-escalate. But don't be too hard on yourself. You're still learning, and its instinctive human behavior. I doubt very much if you'll do it again.

When we're trying to remove barriers to communication, you try and speak to the person where they're at, otherwise you're wasting your time. Keep your language at a level that can easily be understood. You're not trying to show off your intelligence by using big words. Also, learn to look at mistakes as an opportunity to gain experience.

You don't want to look down on people in a critical manner. You want to let them know you're in this together, come hell or high water. You're opening up your body language, you're using the right tone of voice, the right words and proving that even in this tumultuous state, you are a person of reason, a person that can be counted on and a person who understands everything – even anger!

You're also proving that you can communicate evenly and consistently in whatever state this person is in. You're saying in your mind: "In this moment, I'm going to listen to you and I'm going to do whatever I can to help you, believe me.

"Then I'm going to listen some more while you talk yourself through this crisis." In this process, you're going to start using left brain logic and put emotions to bed. What we need to change about ourselves is prejudging someone. You must understand the biases here – implicit, explicit and confirmation bias.

Bias is a belief system that some people, ideas, etc., are better than others. Explicit bias refers to attitudes and beliefs (positive or negative) that we consciously or deliberately have about a person or group. Implicit bias includes attitudes and beliefs (positive or negative) about other people, ideas, issues, or institutions that occur outside of our conscious awareness and control, which affect our opinions and behavior. So, this can be ingrained in our thinking, and we may not even be aware of it.

Confirmation bias is our subconscious way to seek and evaluate information and all sorts of other evidence in to affirm our existing beliefs, ideas, and expectations. Any of these biases will let you pre-judge a situation. These are all barriers to communication!

How can you be listening with an open mind when you may have all these biases crowding about in your head? What you must do is search yourself, thoroughly and honestly. Can you really say that you don't have bias? We all do to some degree or other. Sometimes we have dragged a bias from the pit and examined it, even though it was an onerous thing to do. We never knew it existed, but a stray thought came upon us, and we wondered "Where on earth did that come from?" It came from inside you, that's where. It's something you must be conscious of, all the time, until you can change your thinking.

We are constantly bombarded by social media on all sorts of misinformation and ideas that we never thought twice about, or were enraged at the time, and then forgot about it. Except that we never did. It found a space to let in our minds and moved in without even asking about the rent.

This is much, much more commonplace than you would know. Don't ever think it can't happen to you. We're all fallible, persuadable, and receptive, even when we think that we aren't So, do not judge, my friend. You're on a mission to find justice, so how can you be judgmental at the same time? No sir, you can't. Remember, your mission is not about you, it's about the other person. And our plan to help them get out of their crisis.

With bias in mind, you'll be cutting the person off while they're speaking and then you'll be sprouting off something or other to prove a point. Really? And more than once too. Don't ever be in a rush to speak, and never interrupt the person. You have to listen! Men are terrible at this. We can't help but interrupt, So, I'm calling out all my brothers here!

Make sure you're focused on listening and understanding. Don't be criticizing in your head about what this person has done. You're putting up barriers to understanding and communication. Also, never order the person to do something. Remember the woman who was terminated and wouldn't leave? (*Strategy one*) I know I keep going on about this, but there are moments there which succinctly sum up what we've been talking about through this whole book. When we had our conversation, I listened intently. I paraphrased. I gave her the nods and sounds to let her know that I was listening.

I gave her two options, and an adverse option. She could get an Uber, or I'd drop her at a bus stop. Or, if she still refused to leave, and don't forget she'd been terminated, I would have to call the police and she would be arrested. I never ordered her to do anything, and I never threatened her to do anything. I gave her options with two positive choices (one negative) and empowered her to choose. A barrier to communication can be when you're ordering the person to do something, or if you're threatening a course of action. I didn't do either. I never threatened her with the police. I just gave her the facts.

The facts were the options I gave her. The ONLY options I could give her. Also, never minimize how a person is feeling. This ties into the sympathy versus empathy debate. Like the gentleman who had lost his employment at the manufacturing company (*Strategy four*). He was in crisis. He had lost his job, he had kids to feed and a home he could well lose. What was he to do? How can you minimize the way that this guy was feeling? How would you feel in a similar situation? There's no way we can wave a magic wand and fix everything.

It's what we'd like to do, for sure. But the world is full of sad, awful tales. How someone feels is how someone feels. You can't always change that. You can't offer him another job and a guarantee that his kids would be fed and schooled, and he wouldn't lose his home. It's impossible for you to do. So, what do you do? You shower him with empathy.

If he begins arguing about the unfairness of the world, all you can do is agree. That's a fact. He should go for counselling, but that's not going to fix any of the issues. It could make him feel better. Or not. When you feel you must argue a point with someone because there are blocks you can't move past, there is no winner or loser. Don't argue a point. In conflict it's best not to do this. If you are moving to the point of argument, you're moving past de-escalation techniques into a territory you don't want to be in at all. Know when it is time to move on rather than argue. Also, avoid language that could be seen as confrontational. Words in this category include "I can't" "We don't" "You must."

You should be using cooperative words like "I don't think I can" "We usually don't" "You might try." The most defined words in this category are statements – "What I can do is call you an Uber" "We can't stay here. Let's go somewhere more private," "Let's try this," "Let's look at this," "We can't help you here," "I can't help you here today. You've been terminated. I can't change that, but let's try this attorney out there. They may be able to help you if you feel you have been wrongly dismissed." I was never confrontational. I was positive. I gave solid options which she may not have liked, but I couldn't change that. Everything I did aided communication.

You could find many more situations in which you are called to prove your merit, prove you've got what it takes, prove that empathy is imbedded in you. These are not clichés. They're full-blooded facts. You can embrace it. Or not. It's a demanding job. But you've certainly got what it takes!

THE CHURCHMAN, THE GANG, AND THE COP

It took a leader of a church safety program to defuse an explosive situation between the police and an armed gang. Thanks to his quick thinking and skills, a looming disaster was averted.

Frank Rice is 72 years old and spent much of his early career working with the FBI as a civilian counterintelligence officer. He later moved into security printing and in his retirement, he serves as the leader of his church safety program. Frank shared a story of de-escalation at the end of a church meeting on a Monday night.

Frank was at a new church plant in an area of Minneapolis, Minnesota that had a high crime rate and low-income households. Gangs on street corners was commonplace and for most, it was an intimidating place to be.

One Saturday evening he was finishing up at church when a group of women walked past him. He was standing outside the church talking with someone when all of a sudden, the group of women came running back towards him. With Frank being a former counterintelligence officer and with a career in safety, he was never one to shy away from a situation and do what is right. So, he stopped one of the women running to find out what had happened.

The women, who were church attendees, told Frank that they had returned to their cars in a nearby parking lot and found a group of what they described to him as gang members standing close by. "They had found them intimidating and so had run away,"

Frank being Frank couldn't leave the women stranded, so he went to investigate. What I like about this part of the story is that it shows even at 72, Frank was a person who knew you had to be proactive, and a swift response was often the best way to resolve conflict rather than to let it fester. When Frank walked over to the group, he found around 10 gang members and immediately saw that three of them were armed. In Minnesota it is not against the law to carry a gun in public if you have a permit. If you have been charged and convicted of a felony crime you are prohibited from obtaining a permit. Gangs like these whose lives revolved around crime were unlikely to have obtained their guns legally.

Frank instantly went into de-escalation mode and began to remove the communication barriers that had sprung up, and he explained who he was. He said he worked for a local church down the street, and they would be welcome to stop by for free food and refreshments.

In taking this approach, Frank demonstrated to them that he posed no threat. Once he had established rapport, he went on to say that some women were trying to get back to their cars and when they saw this group of gang members, had been intimidated and had run away.

The person who Frank describes as being the leader of the gang said to him "Okay, we will give you a free pass." This situation, full of tension, could easily have been the trigger for escalation. What is quite common in most conflict situations, someone must be assertive, to be the "winner."

Frank thanked them for allowing them to pass, keeping the advantage with the gang members. Again, this was a great way to remain neutral and show it isn't about winning and losing.

After some passive conversation, Frank offered to prayer over the 10 men, and they seemed to like that idea. After 10-15 minutes of talking with the gang, Frank returned towards the area where the women were congregating to tell them that he had spoken with the gang members and that it would be okay for them to return to the parking lot, get into their cars and leave.

No sooner had Frank said this when he now saw eight of the gang members go sprinting past him away from the area. Frank was surprised as only a few moments earlier he had been praying over these men. He was intrigued as to what happened, so he returned to the area where the men had been.

He saw there were only two gang members left who were getting into an argument with a Minneapolis cop, who was sitting in his car. Frank approached one of the gang members who he had earlier pegged as being the leader and said "What's changed? When I left, you were in good spirits and now you're shouting and screaming at this police officer." The leader of the gang said to Frank: "This cop says it looks like were up to something, but we were just hanging out."

The cop in the car shouted back: "You do look like you're up to something!" which sent the guy over the edge again and the shouting and arguing between the gang member and the cop intensified. Frank made the decision to stand in-between where the gang member was stood, and the police officer who was sat in his car. Frank looked the leader of the gang in the eye and said, "Let it go, no one is going to win this argument." Frank then turned to the police officer in the car, told him who he was, and said "Let it go."

Frank knew that these interactions almost never ended well so he hoped to appeal to the good nature of both men. Frank does not know what would have happened if he hadn't intervened, saying he will never know but these kinds of interactions most often end badly. The two gang members did take Frank's advice and walked away from the situation. Frank said the police officer thanked him for his help.

Like with the gang members, Frank told the cop of the church down the street and that he would be welcome for food. The cop said "You know Frank, I've seen so much; I've seen kids their age with their guts hanging out. Frank could see this young cop was at breaking point. Minneapolis is a boiling point for these young cops and after George Floyd's death in 2020, everyone was on edge.

Some teachings from this story. It can end positively by removing communication barriers. It's a case (isn't it always?) of lost in translation. Think quickly. Speak with the authority of a person who knows what they are speaking about! Both sides can be triggered and escalate. The gang members couldn't be seen to losing face and held ownership of their turf. The solo cop was triggered as he didn't want to show weakness or compromise with how he treated these gang members

Whereas Frank used good de-escalation. He didn't take the situation personally. He demonstrated good skills in building rapport. He didn't make it about a winner and a loser. He also presented himself as the wise old man, using his experience as his advantage. He brought a calmness to the situation.

Not once did he raise his voice. His only intent was to resolve the situation peacefully. He could sense that this cop was at breaking point and most probably wasn't in the right mindset to de-escalate. Either he never knew how to or saw the situation as an inevitable highly charged situation he had to grasp forcefully.

If he knew it or not, the cop's behavior and spoken words were actually escalating the gang members until Frank intervened. Someone had called the cops. The cop knew that he was going into the situation with a position of disadvantage. There were 10 gang members, which could have been intimidating for him. He also took a different stance on the situation by being accusatory, telling the men "They looked like they were up to something," which came over as completely untrusting. Believing or knowing some of them would be armed is most probably the reason that he stayed in the car. This felt safer than confronting the gang face-to-face.

Recap: It's an art to know how to use de-escalation conversational methods to great effect, but the more you do it, the more accustomed and confident you become. Learn the effects that bias can have by bringing in a judgmental attitude on your part. Remember the "I" and "You" words that can have a detrimental or positive effect on your de-escalation attempt. Know what can trigger instability and anger and what can deflate anxious situations.

STRATEGY NINE - REMEMBER PERSONAL SAFETY

#When Words Fail #Detailed Profile #Give Person Space #If Possible, Pacify #Frustration Triggers #Give Attacker Advantage #Acting Out Anger #Non-Retaliation Best #Desfuse Irrational Thinking #Don't Let Guard Down

What happens when you land up in an adverse situation which has the potential to turn violent? How do you respond? This book is not meant to be a manual on these events but must indeed highlight such possibilities.

JIM – AND THE STRANGER IN THE CHURCH

Coming upon an intruder in a church office, this security director didn't have time to collect his thoughts before being tackled to the floor.

I'd like to begin with a story about a good friend of mine, Jim Theis, who found himself in exactly this kind of situation. He's now the security director of our church, but at the time of the event he was the facilities manager. One afternoon, he was at the church.

He went into a room behind the Worship Center and saw a person there acting strangely. People do not generally go into this room, as it's like a private church space. Anyway, there he was, 19-20 years-old, tall, and skinny. They stood, looking at each other. From his startled look and body language, Jim figured his intentions weren't spiritual. He said it seemed that he was on drugs or suffering from some type of mental illness, but he was startled and looked menacing.

Jim didn't have many options and didn't want to instigate violence. He had walked into a room and appeared to have caught a robber in mid-flow. Jim was blocking the door, so it was the robber who had the choice. Be detained and arrested or assault Jim, so he attacked Jim. They fell on the floor. The attacker got up and fled, leaving Jim on the floor, shaken, and bruised. Thankfully, he was not seriously injured.

So, why tell this story? Well, we've discussed stages of anger. What we haven't covered is when words alone can't de-escalate the person in crisis or when you find yourself in a position of danger. The person could be chemically and emotionally impaired and dangerous. So, what do you do?

You don't have to be someone's punching bag! However, when violence seems inevitable, as in Jim's case, there's no way that you can de-escalate someone with your words and behavior.

Can you imagine if you were suddenly attacked? If you haven't signed on at your local martial arts center, think of how you might defend yourself if you don't have the right skills? It's my hope and prayer that you never find yourself in that kind of situation, but in today's volatile world, anything's possible.

You are often called to de-escalate highly emotional and distressed people, and in that kind of situation, violence is an ever-present reality. What you should always do, first things first, is a basic safety risk assessment. Have you got a detailed profile of the person you are trying to de-escalate?

This profile could include a history of violent behavior (although there could always be a first), and physical characteristics. You must consider everything that is known about this person. Would this person be carrying a weapon? How would you know?

If you get into a situation like Jim's, what would you have done? Being unprepared gives you an immediate disadvantage, but that doesn't mean you should just give up!

A simple de-escalation technique that we can use is to give the person space, so they don't feel trapped. This will only heighten and aggravate the situation even further if they feel closed in. With Jim, there wasn't any way to give any breathing space to his attacker. There was only one door, and that was the one he had just opened. I would say, allow the person to have the door. That's the expression I use when you should stand back and allow the person to leave unchallenged. No one has lost or won anything, and that's not the point. The point is that you can be left unscathed as the person you're confronting can run out of the doorway, which you have already vacated.

Always put the would-be attacker in the position of advantage. They can leave if you've allowed them to have the door. You can even smile and show them the door. Like "It's all good. Just leave now, no harm done."

After all, they're not likely to have stolen the crown jewels, and anything this kid had stolen Jim could replace through insurance. So, don't aggravate, but pacify rather. If you're shown surprise, show acceptance and warmth. Every situation is different though. What worked for situation A, may be wrong in situation B. I urge you to read the experience below written by an esteemed psychotherapist on how to deal with physical attacks and proves that you DON'T have to retaliate physically!

The following is a blog written by Toby Ingham entitled *Surviving Attacks in Psychotherapy*, from www.psychotherapy.net It is an excellent site to visit for knowledge on how to respond to many incidents with counseling. It is obviously aimed at professional counselors but has the same pertinence for de-escalators.

A VERY ANGRY YOUNG MAN – AND ME

Here's a story how a psychotherapist was tested with aggressive and attacking behavior.

"The sound of gravel being ripped from my drive is that of an angry 25-year-old man leaving his session with me. He is furious, and though he sat through the final minutes of the session with his emotions firmly in check, they spilled out as soon as he left.

"He is angry with me because I have tried to find out why he walked out of therapy with me three months ago with no warning, and why he wants to come back now. He is here because it is a requirement of his psychoanalytic training, and though he gets some satisfaction from working with me, I don't think he would be here if he wasn't required to be. He is frustrated by my asking about the premature break earlier in the year.

"We are caught in a difficult transference. His acting out, his anger with me, his resistance and refusal to want to find out more about what's going on make things difficult. But it's not going away. By coming back now he has drawn further attention to it. He could have stayed away, and then no questions would have been asked. Not by me! But he's come back because he must for his training.

"I find my practice can run very smoothly (a superstitious side of me prevents me from saying more), but every so often an issue will flare up and the atmosphere is changed. Often clients who are in training prove the most difficult, particularly when they are ambivalent about being in therapy. I think of these experiences as attacks on psychotherapy. Evidence that an attack has been launched is demonstrated by behaviors, and frequently these are behaviors that manifest themselves in terms of boundary or therapeutic frame issues.

"In this example, someone breaks off therapy and then expects to come back with no reference being made to their previous actions. The challenge then is how to find a way of working and thinking these things through with the client without becoming caught up in the attacking behavior. And without, as D.W. Winnicott put it, the psychotherapist retaliating and attacking back.

"When these kind of aggressive and attacking experiences are enacted in psychotherapy, the psychotherapist is tested. The psychotherapist must find a way to keep working with the experience. And as they try to, the client finds more ways of provoking the therapist to retaliate, but retaliation might be fatal to the therapy. It might prove that the client is as unlovable as they already think themselves to be. It might lead to the end of the work. It might prove very hard on the psychotherapist's sense of their own professional identity.

"So, in the sessions that follow I have to find ways, despite the provocations, of developing the therapeutic relationship, trying to develop the relationship so that the client may come to lower their defenses and that in time, the client may become interested in the complicated dynamics that are at work.

"If this can happen, and the therapy can survive the attack, then the client may develop the sense that this therapeutic relationship is not like other murky, unfair, and repressive relationships that they have or had, perhaps with their father. They may come to see that in their therapeutic work with me, they are outside of that original destructive parental paradigm. The negative paternal transference might be resolved. This could then be the beginning of profound change.

"The attack, however, it comes, could be a gateway to change. A gateway out of the stuck world of unhappy relating that the client has lived in. This may be what the client has come to therapy to resolve, although they don't know that yet. The only problem is that the attack is real and happening right now. And the client's way of finding opportunities to provoke the therapist into an uncharacteristic act of rejection are very hard to predict and can be very hard to work with and survive.

"In the case of this particular client, it took some time for his anxiety and his aggressive and attacking behaviors and defenses to be contained within the therapy so that we could think about them together. This seemed to coincide with a more measured approach to his driving. I have gained from my experiences of surviving these kinds of attacks without retaliating- they are always very hard work. They are an occupational hazard." ©Toby Ingham. 2018

You could do well to take the above story to heart. How well do you know the phenomenon of situational awareness? It's a fascinating subject which I'm going to explore in another book about the subject. It focuses on personal safety in many situations and forms - but the underlying factor is - how well are you prepared for any attack? You think you know the situation. You've been in this situation many times before. But look around you. Is there anything lying around that you could defend yourself with in a moment of attack?

Physical attacks can happen in the blink of an eye, especially in the situations you find yourself in when you are talking with people. Have you checked if there's an exit nearby? Could you defend yourself with the very chair you're sitting on? You may have to. Have you ever thought of such things? That the person (whom you don't know at all) could suddenly lunge at you with a knife? How easy is it to slip from awareness to complacency?

It's very, very easy indeed. In that state, people and procedures sail on smoothly by.

Until they don't. Things you are used to suddenly become the unknown. Then you become fully awake. Which is how you should have been from step one. Complacency is the doomsday state. Remember that.

You can't always tell at first glance what a person is really like. They can appear subdued one moment, and very volatile the next. Always be prepared. Don't go into a de-escalation situation when you are distracted in any way. Don't be thinking about what you're going to be doing tonight, have you completed what has to be done for this afternoon's meeting, or whatever. You should be focused on the de-escalation and your heart, mind and soul should be focused on that mission.

Always, always, always be focused. If not, you're letting that person down as well as yourself. Always look the person in the eye, be attentive and paraphrase to show you are listening. This will defuse someone's irrational thinking, which might have also included a physical attack.

Notice if the person's demeanor changes, if their body language changes and if their assertive nature changes. You will then be able to respond appropriately and differently because they have become open and receptive.

Don't ever get caught off-guard. You could miss golden opportunities as well as subtle signs that the person could become threatening. You must learn how to judge moods and how to switch gears just like that.

This is what de-escalation is about. Being on your toes doesn't mean you have to be a ballet dancer, but it does mean you have to be always super-aware. Even when you've thought that the person is de-escalated – actually, especially if you think that you have de-escalated – because that's when you relax and let your guard down. No, no, no. Be alert. The only time that you ever let your guard down is when that person you have been de-escalating walks out of your office, or you walk out of their home or business.

In reading this chapter you should be a little concerned about your safety, as you should be, BUT not scared. I've mentioned martial arts because besides the fact they provide you with great self-help techniques in times of physical crisis, they also help tremendously in awareness and focus techniques.

The person you're seeing may well be emotionally or chemically impaired, so you start off with a disadvantage. If any physical trouble rears its head, the simple thing to do if, like me, you are into soccer, you kick as high as you possibly can. For me, if I have to defend myself, I kick, and kick hard with my left leg. I know that I wouldn't want to be on the receiving end of one of those! That's why I've mentioned defensive classes, because you learn to kick and punch just as hard there. That can take someone completely off guard and they quickly forget about attacking you.

The same goes if I have to take a swing at someone. I've had good practice with golf. It has strengthened my arms and hands. So, know what your strongest arm or leg is! The way to manage threatening attacks, if possible, is by de-escalating verbally out of the situation. It could be the most highly charged situation you've ever been faced with. If you think that you can cope with this like that psychoanalyst, then by all means put yourself to the test.

Remember, you must have trained fully for situations like this. If you're a total pacifist at heart and the thought of harming someone makes your blood run cold, then verbal de-escalation is your best choice. However, if your life is truly at stake, you will have to put pacifism aside for the sake of a good punch or hefty kick.

Recap: Your safety is paramount. You may be able to verbally de-escalate a threatening and explosive situation, or you may have to become physical if you are

attacked. You would do well to sign up for some martial arts classes. They are excellent in physically preparing you for attacks and give you mental awareness and focus techniques.

STRATEGY TEN- KNOW IF YOU'RE THE RIGHT PERSON

#Practice Makes Perfect #Not Me, But Them #Realistic Expectations #Learn from Failure #Slap Down Ego #Give Dignity, Respect #Forgiveness #Tongue A Powerful Sword

It's all about the person in crisis. Right time, right person, right place. If these three situations flow effortlessly together, then whoever's best suited to de-escalate the person should do so. It's always key to remember it's not about you. It's about the person in crisis.

If your de-escalation is not working, it could be time to step aside and let someone else try. Don't take it as a personal thing. It's not about the ego. It's not about you. Think about the school story where the public safety manager wasn't getting anywhere. He had to step aside and let someone else handle the explosive situation.

The manager, though, made the big mistake of making it about himself and sarcastically told the de-escalator who had taken over that he had been "too soft" on the kid. It's not about winning and losing a battle. It's finding a road that rises to meet the person and offering help and support. Ego rage can be quiet and simmering, or it could explode like a volcano. You must have nerves of steel in situations like this. Remember, practice makes perfect. You see, the ego is a silent partner at most times. It's also invisible. So, you tend not to think about it. It's also devious and will rise up from nowhere and you're like "Whoa! Where did that come from?"

I remember when I was a police officer, I was called to a fight outside a bar. Everyone was drunk. As any de-escalator will know, finding the voice of reason in a situation like this is virtually impossible. One of the inebriated people took an instant dislike to me because of my skin color is black. He immediately launched into a tirade of racial slurs. It was easy for me to become irate and get agitated. This is how fights normally begin. I reminded myself, the situation was about him, not me. He was overstepping the boundaries. Was I going to do the same? I asked myself if I was the right person at the right time? At the right place? I had white co-workers with me who could deal with this situation. If I dealt with it, it could have easily escalated. I set myself boundaries that I wasn't going to tolerate this.

So, I removed myself and let my co-workers resolve it. They understood that it was a perfectly natural thing to do. Maybe if the person had been sober, there may have been an opportunity to find the voice of reason. When someone is making it about race. Finding reason will be incredibly challenging with that level of distraction and bias!

These are the kinds of thoughts that arise when you know it's time to stand back. Maybe? Could I? If only? Leave those thoughts be. It's disastrous for you. End of story. I would encourage you to do the same. There could be someone with you who would resonate more with this kind of person and achieve a breakthrough, but it may well not be you.

Remember, changing patterns of behavior is hard at the best of times. Hold realistic expectations. If you believe that you can't do it, let someone else try but don't feel like you don't have what it takes. Of course, you do. Like anything, sometimes life throws you a curve ball and it hits where it hurts. You may just not be the right person and that's when you step aside. You soon get yourself together and get involved another time.

Also, your advice alone may not change a person's behavior. If it doesn't work, it does not mean you've failed. You have all the tips and tools to execute a sold crisis de-escalation, and you've used them successfully over and over. Always, there is the possibility that it may not work, but the successes you've scored far outweigh the failures. You learn from failure. I find that a positive thing. You first see it differently and are down in the dumps because you couldn't get a breakthrough.

Let that emotion come and go, as you must get on with other things. Start seeing that "failure" is a growth trigger. That's the best teacher ever. You start to realize that maybe things could have been done differently and you try it out. You don't know what you're capable of until you try.

Experience is a great teacher! If you're just starting out with de-escalation or honing your skills, be prepared for let-downs. But if you continue using the techniques in this book, you will reap rewards. As you become more confident, you grow.

You know that changing someone's behavior is not the easiest thing in the world, although it is possible. It depends on the de-escalation situation you find yourself in. Routinely, it's hard work. You're trudging up a hill. But keep on, the top is in sight. I've been doing this for some 20 years, and I still get it wrong sometimes.

The following is a perfect story about being the right person at the right time.

FRANK WAS THE RIGHT PERSON AT THE RIGHT TIME

A situation involving a teen and his mother threatened to get out of control and would have had it not been for the calm intervention of a Frank.

At Frank Rice's church in Elk River Minnesota, they host teenagers involved with the national non-profit program Adult and Teen Challenge, which is focused on people who have battled drug and alcohol addiction.

Towards the end of the program, there is a ceremony where all the teens who finish the treatment program invite friends and family to the occasion. At one such ceremony, 15 kids graduated from the program. Frank was inside the church when someone called and told him he needed to come outside quickly because there was a situation unfolding.

Frank went outside to find around 30 people watching a 15-year-old arguing with his mother. Frank listened for a while to get a feel for what was happening. When he had heard enough, he said to the kid: "What I'm hearing is you don't want to go back to 'that place.' Is that right?" What Frank did was paraphrase, which demonstrated he was interested and listening to what the kid had to say. Frank asked: "Where is it that you don't want to go back to?" The kid replied: "To treatment."

Frank used a technique to move the kid's thinking from the right side (emotional) to the left side (logic) by asking him: "What are you getting out of treatment?" The kid explained that he felt he didn't need the program anymore. Frank asked him where he was from, to which he replied "Michigan."

Frank then got him to see the reality of the situation. "We're in the middle of nowhere in Minnesota, so if you don't travel back with your mom to Michigan, how are you going to get home?" Frank painted the reality of the situation and let the kid use logic to see he was overreacting and that this was a conversation for another day.

So, in this story, we learned it's key that if you don't have the skills to de-escalate, raise the alarm and find someone with those skills – such as Frank. We saw that Frank used some pertinent questions to get the kid to move from emotion (right brain) to logic (left brain). This is the time to be purposefully intentional with your words and not escalate the situation by saying something wrong.

The first three-to-five seconds is where your judgment is most clouded. Be mindful of the situation facing you. Frank drowned out the noise of the people watching. Take heed of this quote: "Don't listen to the people in the stands when you're in the arena."

Frank was calm throughout, which is essential. He used paraphrasing. "Where is it you're trying to get back to?" showed the kid he was listening. This is a simple, yet very pertinent example, of what to do in situations that are quite ordinary yet could escalate into something devastating.

Universal truths on interaction

One of the finest books I've read on de-escalation is *Verbal Judo (The Art of Persuasion)* by George G Thompson, Ph.D. If you can get your hands on this, do so. I read it in one sitting, in about 2 hours.

In his work, Dr. Thompson describes the "Five Universal Truths" of human interaction, as follows:

1. All people want to be treated with dignity and respect.
2. All people want to be asked rather than told to do something.

3. All people want to be informed as to why they are being asked or ordered to do something.
4. All people want to be given options rather than threats.
5. All people want a second chance when they make a mistake.

He speaks a lot about respect, understanding, and forgiveness. He says we should approach missions "tactically," and must speak to gain compliance, develop cooperation, or work in collaboration. It's hard not to get caught up in the situations he describes. Although most of them will not pertain to you, you can grab onto the basics of civility, empathy, and understanding when you're dealing with any situation.

Dr. Thompson makes an interesting observation about the tongue being like a powerful sword, and that's exactly what it is. Weapons can harm physically, but the emotional content that words carry cannot be matched by anything else. They can wound, devour, and destroy. They are the most powerful thing on earth, yet, without a second thought, people open mouths and spout words that can damage and destroy you.

Dr. Thompson writes: "Was your tongue cocked?" (And ready to fire?). The tongue, he argues, is the weapon we use in de-escalation the most. It can establish rapport and empathy, which form the basis of our conversations. It can also destroy any progress you may have built. Dr. Thompson explains:

"Developing mind-mouth harmony is the greatest skill in the world, because if you make a mistake with either, you can find yourself in serious personal danger. You can lose a marriage, stall a career, instigate violence, lose your credibility, alienate people, and lose friends."

Dr. Thompson made mistakes all the time, but he never dwelt on them, though. So, if you start de-escalating someone and realize this one is not for you, apologize to the person. I've found the best thing to say is: "I'm sorry. I think there may be a conflict of interest here. May I introduce Peter, who will take care of you from here..."

I've never had a problem with this, and I've taken over for many people. Are you too proud to say this and start bumbling your way through, making a bigger mess of things than what you found when you first came in? Don't be. You know what happened with pride. How was the fall? And never forget the de-escalator motto – it's not about you.

Recap: Remember, it's not about you. It's about the person in crisis. Don't be afraid to step aside and let someone else take over if you realize that they could

be suited to this particular situation. It does not make you less of a competent de-escalator, but rather a much better one. Also, never underestimate the power of words. They can be a double-edged sword, so be careful how you use them.

EPILOGUE

There's a lot to ingest in this book, but make no mistake, there is everything in here for you to learn and be successful in de-escalation. Actually, to me, it's always been much more than just a job or role de-escalating conflict. I've never looked back on any de-escalation in the police or my personal life and thought: "I don't know why I'm the person in the middle of this. I enjoy teaching how to avert danger and harm. For me, it's a passion."

The simple six-step process

I would like to bring the book to a close with this simple six-step step process that you can use when you're first engaged with a person in conflict you're trying to de-escalate. It is designed for people in the workplace but can easily be adapted for you.

Step One – Introduction.

This is simply saying "Hello, my name is Simon. I'm the CEO of Kingswood Security Consulting."

Step Two – The reason for the conversation.

Explain the reason why you are there, "I hear you're looking to talk to someone about an issue. It could be about the delivery of our product…."

Step Three – Ask relevant questions.

"How can I help you with this issue…can you tell me what the cause of the disruption was….. I can see you're highly emotional…tell me what you're in crisis about and we can take it from there."

Step Four – Stop and Listen.

Now use your active listening. Most people don't listen. They want to talk, talk, talk. Not you. Remember to listen to understand, so listen up!

Step Five – Give positive choices.

We know this person is escalated and is in crisis. Do a quick mini brainstorm in your mind. Be creative. What could those positive choices be? How did you fix this problem before? Is there a better way of doing it?

So, we will have listened, we're going to give some positive choices. Then we'll give one bad option in detail, making it unappealing. Remember, the first story (don't sigh – there's everything you need in this one story). I gave the lady who had been terminated at work two good options. The last one was – "You can't stay here. So, I'm going to call law enforcement and you will be arrested for trespass." OR the good options - "You can let me call an Uber, or we can take you to a bus stop."

Step 6 – Appropriate close.

"I really hope you can move on from this situation. Thank you for your time and thank you for allowing me to listen. You want an Uber. Certainly. It should be here in 20 minutes. Can we go down together?"

Every situation is going to be different, but you have a standard template above that you can adapt to your needs. Here is my closing advice, follow the steps in this book and have fun with it. Not everything in life has to be so serious, there is often laughter in finding out what works and what doesn't. Maybe one day you will be writing your own book on your de-escalation endeavors.

My hope in writing this book is that you just take these teachings and try to make the world a safer place AND support those people in crisis that need to just let a little bit of air out of the balloon, as we all do on occasion – even me!

Happy de-escalating my friends. My wishes and prayers reach out to you.

Simon Osamoh

ABOUT THE AUTHOR

Simon Osamoh is a British-American and founder of Kingswood Security Consulting, a Minneapolis based security risk management firm.

He first moved to the United States in 2011 to Head Counter Terrorism at Mall of America. The largest shopping and entertainment complex in North America where he oversaw counterterrorism and the internationally recognized behavior threat assessment team.

Simon spent 14 years as a Detective in England working serious and organized crime. One of his notable cases includes working with the British Security Services during the investigation of the "liquid bomb terrorism plot", which changed aviation security regulations worldwide.

He is the author of three books and his work on conversational interviewing featured in the award-winning book *How to Stop a Mass Shooting Epidemic* by

Dr. James Densley and Dr. Jillian Peterson of the Violence Project.

You can connect with Simon at info@kingswoodsc.com

Printed in Great Britain
by Amazon